Healing Power of
GEMS
And
Stones

Healing Power of Gems *and* Stones

V. Rajsushila
Gemologist

Published by:

F-2/16, Ansari Road, Daryaganj, New Delhi-110002
☎ 011-23240026, 011-23240027 • *Fax:* 011-23240028
Email: info@vspublishers.com • *Website:* www.vspublishers.com

Regional Office : Hyderabad
5-1-707/1, Brij Bhawan (Beside Central Bank of India Lane)
Bank Street, Koti, Hyderabad - 500 095
☎ 040-24737290
E-mail: vspublishershyd@gmail.com

Branch Office : Mumbai
Godown # 34 at The Model Co-Operative Housing, Society Ltd.,
"Sahakar Niwas", Ground Floor, Next to Sobo Central, Mumbai - 400 034
☎ 022-23510736
E-mail vspublishersmum@gmail.com

Follow us on:

All books available at **www.vspublishers.com**

© Copyright: V&S PUBLISHERS
ISBN 978-93-813843-6-7
Edition 2015

The Copyright of this book, as well as all matter contained herein (including illustrations) rests with the Publisher. No person shall copy the name of the book, its title design, matter and illustrations in any form and in any language, totally or partially or in any form. Anybody doing so shall face legal action and will be responsible for damages.

Printed at : Param Offseters Okhla New Delhi-110020

Contents

Preface vii

1. Influence of Gems 9
2. Mystical and Divine Powers of
   Precious Gems 17
3. Most Powerful Semi-precious
   Gem Stones 23
4. Selection of Gem Stone According to the
   Zodiac Sign and Stars 29
5. Selection of Gem Stones According
   to the Stars 35
6. Selection of Gem According
   to Numerology 41
7. Gems and Numerology 47
8. Selection of Gems Based on First Letter
   of the Name 53
9. Pooja for Stones–Precious and
   Semi-precious Gems 59
10. Gems and Diseases 71
11. Gems for Professional Success 75
12. Auspicious Times and Metals for
    Wearing Gems 77
13. Crystals and Gems for the
    New Millennium 79

PREFACE

From time immemorial gems have been used by people in different ways. It has curative power as well as the power to pour in fortune and drive away the evil of our planetary position. Certain gems and stones have magical powers of healing and changing the fortune. Gems have made lives of many individuals happier and more successful. They are widely used to get benefit from the planets as these little gems serve as a never-ending source of the rays of the planet and continue even after years. According to astrology and numerology, gems counteract the bad effects of planets and bring us luck, fortune, prosperity, status, knowledge, concentration, good health, name and fame.

In this book, I have tried to give a detailed description of various gems and their qualities, including not only 'Nav Ratnas', the nine precious gems, but also many substitute gems, that do wonders when they are worn.

Appropriate care should be taken while choosing a particular gem. In this book, I have discussed in detail the various methods of selecting gems. Gems can be selected on the basis of our Zodiac or the star we are born under. Gems can also be chosen according to our name's first letter, date and month of birth.

It will be interesting to note that some gems have with them the perennial power to push us forward in an occupation. Many professionals, businessmen and service persons have benefited by wearing the gem which helps them go up in their respective occupations, multiple profits. Gems also lessen the scope of loss and protect them from all adversaries. A person aspiring to join films can wear Cat's Eye or Garnet by selecting it according to his date of birth or star and get to the top position. Similarly, there is a gem for every occupation.

I have also discussed the effects of gems on health. How efficiently our health problems can be minimised by imputing a particular colour in our body and adjusting the colour rays by wearing the correct gems, has been clearly explained.

Gems work magically and do wonders when we make the ring at the appropriate period of the transit of planets, and after doing the necessary rituals.

I have tried to give detailed description of selection and benefits of gems in this book to derive maximum results for better life and prosperity.

–**Author**

1

Influence of Gems

Gems are found in almost all parts of the world. India has been very rich in terms of gem stones. They are found in abundant quantities in the country, especially in Madhya Pradesh, Orissa, Bihar, Maharashtra, Andhra Pradesh, Kerala and Karnataka.

Gem stones are useful for our health, longevity, name, fame, prosperity and fortunes. In ancient times, kings and princes used to keep gem stones in their treasury to ensure prosperity. They would also set these gem stones in jewellery and wear them with pride.

Gem stones have different effects on different people. There have been instances where childless women after wearing a particular gem began conceiving. Some kings got victorious in the battles by wearing some prescribed gems. Certain gem stones are known to have cured people of some dreaded diseases. As a result of these beneficial effects, some ancient scholars began conducting research about these stones. Their experiments proved the beneficial effects of gems and stones. This inspired different types of studies about gems, which were developed as *Science of Gemology*. Thus, Varaha Mihira, one of the greatest ancient scholars, wrote a book about gems called *Ratna Dipika*.

Our ancient scholars also used gem stones in the medicines in the form of *Bhasmas* to cure many diseases.

Wearing correct gem stones at suitable times has proved very helpful in achieving success in wealth, health and succeeding in other matters. There are so many gem stones, but only nine gem stones are considered as 'Precious Gems'.

These are called the 'Nav Ratnas'. Although there are many gem stones in the world, these nine gem stones have been given great importance by our ancient scholars. These are powerful gems, which reflect the strength of planets, and also produce changes in our body. Their corresponding planets are listed on page 12.

The nine precious gems identified in this respect are Ruby, Diamond, Emerald, Yellow Sapphire, Blue Sapphire, Gomeda, Pearl, Cat's Eye and Coral.

Of all these gems, only Pearl and Coral are taken out from the ocean, while Cat's Eye, Gomeda, Yellow Sapphire, Blue Sapphire, Emerald, Ruby are mined from the earth. The gems found under the earth have mineral content. In fact, each gem has a prescribed content of minerals. Our body requires minerals for growth. If any mineral is deficient in our body, we suffer from ill health, depending upon the extent of the deficiency. To make up for this deficiency physicians advise us to take some medicine, which contains those minerals. If we take such medicines, our ailment would be cured. Similarly, gems, which have certain mineral content, adjust our mineral deficiency and improve our health. Medicines can cure only the physical ailments, whereas gems help us surmount our difficulties, and achieve wealth and prosperity.

Gems have the power to keep a balance among these minerals in our body.

The suitable gem, which we choose to wear, should touch our body. If we wear a suitable gem, the cosmic rays of the planet related to that particular gem, enter our body through that gem and produce good effect on us. Hence, we get success in our life. This is "Good Luck".

How is it possible for a planet to affect a particular individual who has worn its particular gem stone, among crores of people in the world and produce its good effect? How can that planet produce its good effect through a small and tiny gem stone?

This doubt may arise. But then how the television is controlled by remote control; how the rocket and its fixed camera are controlled by electronic computers? In the same manner, planets are also controlled by the gem stones.

The vibrations produced by planets are always negative. But the vibrational power of the gem stone is always positive. When the negative meets the positive, they are both neutralised.

Human beings suffer in three ways—physically, mentally and spiritually. Gems help by transmitting planetary rays into the body of the sufferer. When it is hot Sun or rain, we use umbrella. The umbrella protects us from the rain or hot rays of the Sun. In the same manner, when we use the proper gem, the negative rays of the planets are filtered by it and only the beneficial rays are allowed to enter the body. Thus the gems act as a shield, and guard against the evil influences of the planets.

PLANET	GEM
Sun	Ruby
Moon	White Pearl
Mars	Red Coral
Jupiter	Yellow Sapphire
Mercury	Emerald
Venus	Diamond
Saturn	Blue Sapphire
Rahu	Gomeda
Ketu	Cat's Eye

When radiation is applied to the above listed planetary gem stones, they record the following wave lengths.

No.	GEM	WAVE LENGTH
1.	Ruby	70,000
2.	Pearl	70,000
3.	Red Coral	65,000
4.	Emerald	75,000
5.	Yellow Sapphire	50,000
6.	Diamond	60,000
7.	Blue Sapphire	79,000
8.	Gomeda	70,000
9.	Cat's Eye	70,000

For planetary vibrations, we get the following wave lengths.

No.	PLANET	WAVE LENGTH
1.	Sun	65,000
2.	Moon	65,000
3.	Mars	85,000
4.	Mercury	65,000
5.	Jupiter	1,30,000
6.	Venus	1,30,000
7.	Saturn	65,000
8.	Rahu	35,000
9.	Ketu	35,000

All these planetary vibrations are negative. These negative current waves are neutralised by positive vibrations of the gems.

Gems should be set in rings to enable the planetary rays to pass right through the gem into our body. Numerology can guide a man to select the suitable gem.

Precious and Semi-precious Gem Stones

According to the Indian Gemmology, there are 84 gem stones. Among them, the nine precious stones, namely Ruby, Pearl, Yellow Sapphire, Diamond, Emerald, Blue Sapphire, Red Coral, Gomeda and Cat's Eye have been awarded distinct status. These are called the Nav Ratnas. The other stones are semi-precious stones. Some of the semi-precious stones are also very powerful and they should not be considered as inferior to Nav Ratnas. In hardness, lustre, clarity and radiation some of the semi-precious stones work wonderfully.

Nature of the Precious Stones or Nav Ratnas

1. **Ruby:** This has red colour. Ruby is also found in rose, black, yellow and sky blue colours.
2. **Diamond:** This is found in white, yellow, red, blue and black colours.
3. **Emerald:** It is green in colour. The Emerald of peacock feather colour, parrot colour and grass blade colour, have the best qualities.
4. **Blue Sapphire:** This is found in dark blue, ordinary blue and light blue colours.
5. **Cat's Eye:** This is found in yellowish or blackish colours. The stone has a visible shining band inside, which moves when the stone is turned.
6. **Pearl:** This is found in white, yellow, red or black colours.
7. **Red Coral:** This is found in orange-red colour. White corals are also available.
8. **Yellow Sapphire:** This is found in light yellow colour.
9. **Gomeda:** This is found in honey colour.

Nature of the Most Important and Fortunate Semi-precious Stones

1. **Turquoise:** This is found in light blue colour.
2. **Peridot:** Light green colour.

3. **Tourmaline:** It is available in white, red, green, and blue colours.
4. **Topaz:** This is found in smoky, yellow and golden colours.
5. **Amethyst:** Light violet colour.
6. **Rock Crystal:** It is found in shining white colour.
7. **Moon Stone:** This is found in white cloud colour. There is a shining band inside which rolls when the stone is turned.
8. **Garnet:** This is found in blackish red colour.
9. **Neeli:** This is found in blue colour. It looks like blue Sapphire.
10. **Aquamarine:** Very light green colour.
11. **Jade:** Green colour without shining.
12. **Blood Stone:** Green colour with red spots.
13. **Lapis Lazuli:** Dark blue colour.
14. **Kidney Stone:** Light green colour.
15. **Amber:** Wheat-like colour.
16. **Agate:** This is found in many colours and is considered auspicious by Muslims.
17. **Jaichint:** Orange colour. It is a stone for Rahu.
18. **Green Onyx:** It is in beautiful green colour.
19. **Malachite:** This is in green colour with white strips.

These semi-precious stones can be used as effective substitutes for the nine precious stones.

Nowadays many stones are manufactured through artificial processes and are available in the market. Although artificial gems look like the precious and semi-precious gems, they have no power at all. They cannot do any benefit to the wearer. Only a gemmologist would be able to find the difference, while an ordinary person is unable to detect this.

2

Mystical and Divine Powers of Precious Gems

Nav Ratnas or the nine precious stones—Ruby, Pearl, Yellow Sapphire, Diamond, Emerald, Blue Sapphire, Red Coral, Gomeda and Cat's Eye—have great mystical and divine powers. Their special features have been described here in detail.

1. **Ruby:** Ruby is the stone of the Sun, and protects those who wear it, from the harmful effects of Sun. Ruby is found in red colour, yellow colour, violet mixed red colour, and in rose colour. Ruby will give intelligence and knowledge. The subject would be blessed with children, honoured by others, and receive government favour. Ruby will bestow mental peace, success in politics and educational fields, gains of land and property, comfort of conveyances. Ruby will protect from ill-health and enemies, bring success in administrative fields, freedom from troubles, debts and diseases. It ensures long life, and cures heart diseases.

    Note: Persons born on dates 8, 17, 26, 6, 15 & 24 should not wear Ruby.

2. **Pearl:** Pearls are available in many colours, but of all, white and red coloured pearls are the best. Round pearls are superior. Flat typed

pearls should not be worn. Wearing of Pearl helps the native get freedom from mental disturbances, happiness from mother, success in educational fields, gain of land and house property and conveyances. Pearl ensures good health and long life. It improves finance. With its help one can achieve name, fame and can also be blessed with a male child. It brings success in career, and removes evil effects of bad spirits. Pearl has the power to unite a separated couple. It drives away bad luck and ensures good luck. Pearl cures many diseases like mental disorder, gastric problem, asthma, cough, eye trouble, breathing troubles, and lung disorder.

Note: Pearl should not be worn by persons born on 3, 12, 21, 30, 8, 17, 26 dates.

3. **Yellow Sapphire:** It is available in light yellow or golden colour. It should be heavy, transparent and glittering. Yellow sapphire will make one intellectual, charitable, religiously inclined and respectable towards elders. It ensures wealth, honour, name and fame. It will bless the native with good children. It also acts as a protective charm. It ensures comforts in life. One can fulfil all the desires by wearing yellow sapphire. Those who find obstruction in progress of their educational field, or those who suffer from the difficulties in property matters, should wear yellow sapphire.

Note: Yellow Sapphire should not be worn by persons born on dates 2, 11, 20, 29, 5, 14, 23, 6, 15, 24, 7, 16, 25, 8, 17, 26.

4. **Emerald:** This is a beautiful velvety green colour stone. The Emerald with a deep velvet green to grass green colour, radiant, smooth, transparent

and with bright rays and water mark, and without any dots or spots, is the best and most auspicious gem.

Emerald helps in acquiring wealth and the native would be blessed with children, intelligence and good fortune. It also bestows good health, wealth, longevity, land and property, domestic happiness, a smooth and obstruction-free life. It brings advancement in profession, name, fame and honour.

It drives away evil spirits.

It cures eye diseases.

It controls B.P. and nervous problems.

It turns enemies into friends.

Note: Emerald should not be worn by persons born on dates 3, 12, 21, 30, 9, 18, 27.

5. **Diamond:** Diamonds are white, blue, red and black colour stones.

   It ensures longevity, and advancement in life. It can bless the native with children, happiness, intelligence, name, fame and good fortune. It ensures abundant wealth, and success in all ventures.

   It cures the diseases of kidney and reproductive organs. It drives away evil spirits, and bad effects of evil eyes. It ensures happy married life, possession of jewellery and ornaments, rich dresses, conveyance, comfortable house, birth of good children etc.

   Note: Diamond should not be worn by persons born on dates 1, 10, 19, 28, 3, 12, 21, 30, 9, 18, 27.

6. **Red Coral:** Red Coral, as its name suggests, is generally of red colour. It may even be of orange red colour.

Red Coral will bestow good health, longevity, courage, name, fame and happiness. The native would be blessed with children, intelligence, good fortune and success in professional life. It would also grant land and property, domestic harmony, gains of wealth. It cures all kinds of mental and physical diseases, and difficulties. It saves one from natural calamities like thunder, floods and fires. Its use also helps in removing impediments that could be delaying one's marriage.

Women, who suffered from miscarriages, should wear this for successful delivery.

Note: Red Coral should not be worn by persons born on dates 2, 11, 20, 29, 5, 14, 23, 7, 15, 25, 8, 17, 26.

7. **Blue Sapphire:** This is available in dark, ordinary, or light blue colours. Blue sapphire is ruled by Saturn. It is believed that it gives very beneficial results. But in case it proves unsuitable, it could destroy the life of the native. It has been experienced that sometimes a blue sapphire which is suitable to the nativity, proves very harmful to the native. This is due to some stones, which are born unlucky. Therefore, blue sapphire should only be worn after a trial and got set in the ring only if it does not prove unlucky during the trial period. A trial for about a week should be enough.

After wearing a blue sapphire one gets good servants. The native will always enjoy happiness, prosperity, name, and fame, advancement in the profession, favours from government. It bestows good health, and success in all ventures. The native will get land, building and properties. It also ensures success in politics. One could become either a king or a great scholar by wearing blue sapphire.

Note: Blue Sapphire should not be worn by persons born on dates 1, 10, 19, 28, 2, 11, 20, 29, 3, 12, 21, 30, 4, 13, 22, 31, 9, 18, 27.

8. **Gomeda:** Its colour is like red-coloured smoke. The Ceylon Gomeda is of honey colour.

    Gomeda will bestow good health, win over enemies, and bring wealth and prosperity to its owner.

    It cures skin diseases, gives knowledge, and intelligence. It promotes good education, and ensures improvement in the profession. The native's business would flourish. The adverse effects caused by an evil also vanish. One gets quite active by wearing Gomeda, and gets promotion in the service. It can give unexpected wealth to its wearer. It bestows a very happy life, and the enmity of relatives disappears. Evil spirits go away. It ensures sound sleep and gives peace of mind.

    Note: Gomeda should not be worn by persons born on dates 2, 20, 29, 3, 12, 21, 30, 7, 16, 25, 8, 17, 26, 9, 18, 27.

9. **Cat's Eye:** This is yellowish or blackish in colour. Inside there is a shining band which moves when the stone is turned.

    This is a quick-action gem and restores lost wealth. Poverty and diseases vanish. It ensures victory over enemies and affords protection from enemies. By wearing a Cat's Eye one may be attracted by others. It grants philosophical disposition and activity of the mind. The native gets name, fame and wealth. He who wears this gem, becomes calm, and his anger disappears. He receives the help of relatives and friends. Enemies may bow to him. It works successfully in getting back the loaned money too. It ensures the welfare of the children. Childless person may be blessed with children after wearing this gem. It protects from accident, pimples and skin diseases. It ensures quick marriage.

Note: Cat's Eye should not be worn by persons born on 4, 13, 28, 9, 18, 27.

3

Most Powerful Semi-precious Gem Stones

There are many semi-precious gem stones, which have equally amazing powers to turn one's fortunes. Of all the gems, the following are considered more auspicious and fortunate gems.

These are:

Turquoise, Peridot, Tourmaline, Topaz, Amethyst, Rock Crystal, Moonstone, Garnet, Neeli, Aquamarine, Jade, Blood Stone, Lapis Lazuli, Kidney Stone, Amber, Agate, Jaichint, Green Onyx and Malachite.

1. **Turquoise:** This is one of the semi-precious stones and it was believed that Venus and Saturn are its rulers. Chemically it is the hydrous phosphate of alumina, coloured by a copper compound on account of its water content. A good turquoise is sky blue in colour.

    It emits healing radiation of the shade of greenish-blue. The stone can protect the wearer from injury by falling. It will draw upon itself the evil that threatens its wearer. Unfortunately if any evil is to come to the native, the stone gets broken and the wearer is still protected. It has the power to protect against evils. This gem stone is respected by Muslims. It is also a lover's fortunate gem. It keeps a couple in harmony with each other. It is a fortunate gem for performing quick marriage. It is also lucky for horsemen and riders.

2. **Peridot:** It is greenish in colour. Chemically, it is the silicate of magnesium and iron. It is ruled by the Sun. Like turquoise, it is a fortunate stone for performing quick marriage and protecting the married life. It ensures a happy married life. This gem stone controls the epilepsy disease. It also saves one from poisonous insects. Even if they bite, nothing would happen, and the person would be cured soon.

3. **Tourmaline:** There are different varieties available in different colours. It is the silicate and borate of alumina, magnesia and iron.

   Red, white, green, yellow and blue can be used as substitutes for Ruby, Diamond, Emerald, Yellow Sapphire and Blue Sapphire respectively.

   It improves one's knowledge and promotes good education. It helps the native build good character, respect elders and become responsible.

4. **Topaz:** This stone stands for friendship and fidelity. It is available in white, pink, black, yellow and smoky colours. Yellow Topaz has magical powers. It is good for health. Its use protects one from a sudden or violent death. It is ruled by the Sun. It also helps in toning down negative feelings towards others, and cools down one's temper. It sharpens the intelligence. It drives away nightmares, and brings sound sleep.

Topaz can guard against injury by fire or accidents. It is a good amulet while travelling and helps one to overcome obstacles on the way. It ensures wealth. It cures eye, liver and kidney disorders and also lungs and nasal disorders, throat diseases and asthma.

5. **Amethyst:** This is a variety of quartz. Mars, Saturn and Jupiter rule this semi-precious gem stone. It is a light to dark violet-coloured gem. It works as a very effective substitute for blue sapphire. It is made up of iron and manganese oxides. It is an effective antidote against alcohol and saves one from adverse effects of drunkenness. Amethyst controls violent and angry behaviour. It has the power to control evil thoughts. It protects the person and warns against enemies, sickness and danger. It can ward-off the evil eye, and works as a charm against witchcraft and black magic.

6. **Rock Crystal:** It is white and clear like ice, with a shining white colour. It prevents bad dreams. It fills women's breasts with milk. The rays of the Sun reflected by this crystal have healing power for all eye troubles. These reflected rays should fall only on the body and not in the eyes. It gives good luck, knowledge and wisdom. It has power to cure many diseases and even cancer.

7. **Moon Stone:** It is available in white cloudy colours. Inside the stone there is a glittering band which rolls when the stone is turned. This stone brings good fortune to the native. It has the mystical power of reconciling lovers who had parted in anger. It promises good fortune and success in the affairs of the heart. It can ward off epilepsy, and protect the person against

attack by hidden enemies. It cures mentally disturbed persons, and promotes peace of mind. It is a powerful talisman when there is danger of drowning. This is because of influence of the moon upon the tides. It saves from accident in journey. It grants marital happiness. It brings separated couples together.

8. **Garnet:** Its colour ranges from a fine deep red to a ruby red. Blackish red garnet is regarded as the finest. Garnet ensures the victory of the wearer in the battle when it is used as a bullet. It brings fortune, health, name, fame and honour, and success in travels. It keeps away bad dreams. It gives energy and strength to the body.

   It gives success in the court cases. It cures depression and rheumatism. It controls bleeding.

9. **Neeli:** As its name suggests, it is blue in colour. Saturn exercises power through it. It is the substitute of blue sapphire. It brings success, relief from financial crises and ensures good health to the wearer.

10. **Aquamarine:** This is of very light greenish white colour. It is ruled by Venus and Mars. It is a fortunate stone for lovers. If one presents this to another, it gives them constant mind in love. It protects the sailor in the sea voyage. It promotes education and improves professional prospects.

11. **Jade:** This is of green colour, but without brilliance or lustre. This is a lucky stone by the Chinese, reputed to ensure good health and long life. There are two types of Jade: Jadeite and Nephrite. Jadeite is the silicate of sodium and

aluminium. Nephrite is the silicate of calcium and magnesium. It confers long life and a peaceful end. It is a powerful protector against accidents, diseases, witchcraft. It cures epilepsy and all internal complaints. It cures all diseases of kidney and is often referred to as "The Kidney Stone". It strengthens lungs, heart and vocal organs. It is a powerful antidote against the poisonous bites of snakes and other animals. It relieves palpitations of the heart. It brings good luck.

12. **Blood Stone:** This stone is of dark green colour with blood-like red spots on it. It cures all kinds of complaints wherein there is loss of blood. It cures bleeding. It protects the wearer from deception, and ensures good health.

13. **Lapis Lazuli:** This is a stone ruled by Venus and Saturn. It is a soft stone of dark blue colour. It promotes activeness. One gets success in cases related to land and properties. Chronic diseases, allergies, blood pressure ailments, eye troubles and skin disease may be cured. It brings wealth and property, success in profession and domestic happiness. Women who suffer from stomach pain during the menses period, should wear this. It would cure their stomach-ache and keep them in good health.

14. **Kidney Stone:** Light green in colour, it is worn for disorders of kidney. It cures all kidney disorders and promotes good health.

15. **Amber:** It protects health and reduces goitre. It relieves stomach pain, and improves liver and kidney functioning. It cures teeth disorders, cold and jaundice. It is also a cough-cure. It is especially favoured for toothache, headache and rheumatic pains.

16. **Agate:** These are available in red, yellow and white colours. Red is ruled by Mars, yellow by the Sun and white by Jupiter.

    It ensures happiness and peace of mind. It makes a person brave and courageous. It protects against accidents and troubles like natural calamities. It also brings financial success.

17. **Jaichint:** It is of orange colour. It is ruled by Rahu. It ensures good health, wealth and prosperity. It promotes good sleep. It protects against electrical shock. Diseases like plague, wounds and injuries get cured fast. It cures skin problems.

18. **Onyx:** It is beautiful green in colour. It protects against evil eye. It is a fortunate stone for lovers. It ensures conjugal happiness, and a good married life with understanding between the couple.

19. **Malachite:** It is of dark bluish colour with black or green stripes on it. It is ruled by Mercury & Venus. It is helpful in curing common ailments afflicting babies. It promotes good sleep. In love marriage, if one presents this to one's partner, the wearer of this gem never changes his or her mind, and becomes constant in mind. It drives away evil spirits, and wards off evil eye. It cures troubles related to pancreas, spleen, asthma, menses problems, eye diseases, cholera etc. This is a fortune-giving stone.

4

Selection of Gem Stone According to the Zodiac Sign and Stars

You can select your gem according to your star or Zodiac sign. The Zodiac or a circle is of 360 degree. Each division or a house or Rasi (as known in India) is of 30 degrees. There are 12 divisions of the Zodiac and each has a different ruling planet. The 12 solar months are named after the 12 Zodiac signs. Zodiac is divided into 12 equal divisions of 30 degrees. The 30 degrees is again divided for 2½ stars.

Each star has four pada or parts and 9 such parts are set up for one Rashi or division of Zodiac. Thus each part is of 30 degrees divided by 9 = 3.20 degree.

The following chart is essential for reference. Your Janma Rashi is in accordance with the position of star pada or part. For example, if your star is Krithika 1st part, it is Aries, and if it is Kritika 2nd part, it is Taurus, and so on.

This chart can give you a clear understanding of your Rashi. You would be able to know through your star which Rashi you belong to, and which is your Zodiac sign—and then select your gem accordingly.

1 Aries or Mesha   Degrees

Ashwini	1,2,3,4 parts	
Bharani	1,2,3,4 parts	1 to 30
Krittika	1st part	

2 Taurus or Rishabha   Degrees

Krittika	2,3,4 parts	
Rohini	1,2,3,4 parts	31 to 60
Mrigashira	1,2 parts	

3 Gemini or Mithuna   Degrees

Mrigashira	3,4 parts	
Ardra	1,2,3,4 parts	61 to 90
Punarvasu	1,2,3 parts	

4 Cancer or Kataka   Degrees

Punarvasu	4th part	
Pushyami	1,2,3,4 parts	91 to 120
Aslesha	1,2,3,4 parts	

5 Leo or Simha   Degrees

Makha	1,2,3,4, parts	
Purva Phalguni	1,2,3,4 parts	121 to 150
Uttara Phalguni	1st part	

6 Virgo or Kanya   Degrees

Uttara Phalguni	2,3,4 parts	
Hasta	1,2,3,4 parts	151 to 180
Chitra	1,2 parts	

7 Libra or Tula   Degrees

Chitra	3,4 parts	
Swati	1,2,3,4 parts	181 to 210
Vishakha	1,2,3 parts	

8 Scorpio or Vrichika		Degrees
Vishakha	4th part	
Anuradha	1,2,3,4 parts	211 to 240
Jyeshta	1,2,3,4 parts	

9 Sagittarius or Dhanur		Degrees
Moola	1,2,3,4 parts	
Purvashada	1,2,3,4 parts	241 to 270
Uttarashada	1st part	

10 Capricorn or Makara		Degrees
Uttarashada	2,3,4 parts	
Shravana	1,2,3,4 parts	271 to 300
Dhanishta	1,2 parts	

11 Aquarius or Kumbha		Degrees
Dhanishta	3,4 parts	
Satabhisha	1,2,3,4 parts	301 to 330
Purvabhadra	1,2,3 parts	

12 Pisces or Meena		Degrees
Purvabhadra	4th part	
Uttarabhadra	1,2,3,4 parts	331 to 360
Revati	1,2,3,4 parts	

Details of Zodiac Divisions and How to Select the Gem According to Your Zodiac Sign:

1. **Aries or Mesha:** This is the first Zodiac sign. Its ruler is Mars. The gem of Mars is Red Coral. If Mars is afflicted by other planets or debilitated or posited in the negative place in the horoscope, it may give negative effects. If you wear Red Coral, this can protect from the evil effects of Mars. If Mars is debilitated or in the enemy house, it can lead you to bonded

labour. If you wear Red Coral, you can get scope for doing independent work or get promotion in the work. Red Coral will give mental strength, and the glands will work properly.

2. **Taurus or Rishabha:** This is the second Zodiac sign. This is ruled by Venus. The gem of Venus is Diamond. If Venus is afflicted by other planets, or debilitated, or posited in the enemy house or in negative position in the horoscope, Venus may give unfavourable results. However, use of Diamond can minimize the evil effects of Venus and produce good effects. This will bring wealth, name, fame and prosperity. Even if Venus is posited in good place in the horoscope, wearing of Diamond will enhance the positive effect.

3. **Gemini or Mithuna:** This is the third Zodiac sign. Its ruler is Mercury. The gem of Mercury is Emerald. If Mercury is afflicted by other planets or debilitated, or posited in the enemy house or in negative position in the horoscope, Mercury will give negative effects. The use of Emerald gives strength to Mercury and wards off its evil-effects. It protects the nervous system, and brings success in education and profession. It also helps in turning other's enmity into friendship.

4. **Cancer or Karka:** This is the fourth Zodiac sign. Its ruler is the Moon. The gem of the Moon is Pearl. If the Moon is afflicted, debilitated or posited in the enemy house, or in negative place in the horoscope, it can result in ill-health to mother, lack of concentration, dull-minded personality, gastric troubles, breathing problems and even asthmatic troubles. These ailments may be cured by wearing a Pearl.

Financial success and comfortable life will follow.

5. **Leo or Singha:** This is the fifth Zodiac sign. Its ruler is Sun. The gem of Sun is Ruby. If Sun is afflicted, or debilitated, or posited in the enemy house, or in negative place in the horoscope, it can cause financial hardship, troubles through officials, or workers, heart diseases, etc. Wearing of Ruby reduces these troubles, and gives success in dealing with the Government officials, fame, social success etc.

6. **Virgo or Kanya:** This is the sixth Zodiac sign. Its ruler is Mercury. Its gem is Emerald. Wearing of Emerald will reduce all stomach disorders, and improve knowledge.

7. **Libra or Tula:** This is the seventh Zodiac sign. The ruler of this sign is Venus. Its gem is Diamond. So if Diamond is worn, it improves the financial position, brings promotion and abundant wealth.

8. **Scorpio or Vrishchika:** This is the eighth Zodiac sign. The ruler of this sign is Mars. The gem of Mars is Red Coral. By wearing Red Coral, one can achieve success in finance, and get strength of mind and heart.

9. **Sagittarius or Dhanu:** This is the ninth Zodiac sign. The ruler of this sign is Jupiter. The gem of Jupiter is Yellow Sapphire. If Jupiter is afflicted by other planets, or debilitated, or posited in the enemy's house or in negative position, it can give unfavourable effects. To ward off these effects, one should wear Yellow Sapphire. Through this Jupiter gets strength and brings great fortune. The subject concerned would get good name in the society, live

comfortably, without any diseases, and get name and fame. Even if Jupiter is well posited in the horoscope, wearing of Yellow Sapphire will enhance the good qualities of Jupiter.

10. **Capricorn or Makara:** This is the tenth Zodiac sign. Its ruler is Saturn. The gem of Saturn is Blue Sapphire. If Saturn is afflicted or debilitated, or occupying enemy house or posited in negative position in the horoscope, it can produce unfavourable results. Wearing of Blue Sapphire will minimize the evil effects of Saturn, and produce good effects. It helps in doing away with laziness and the subject becomes active mentally and physically. He gets success in the land and property cases. Unexpected money comes his way.

    Even if Saturn is posited well in the horoscope, wearing of Blue Sapphire will enhance the good effects of Saturn.

11. **Aquarius or Kumbha:** This is the eleventh house of Zodiac sign. Its ruler is Saturn. Blue Sapphire is its gem. Wearing of Blue Sapphire brings success and prosperity.

12. **Pisces or Meena:** This is the twelfth sign of Zodiac. Its ruler is Jupiter. Its gem is Yellow Sapphire. Wearing of Yellow Sapphire brings good fortune to the wearer.

A planet if posited in an unfavourable house, or debilitated or afflicted, will lose its strength and produce unfavourable results. Wearing of a particular gem connected to that planet will ward off these bad effects and produce good effects. Even when the planet is posited powerfully in a favourable house, and is a fortune giver in the horoscope, wearing of suitable gem enhances its good qualities and produces more beneficial effects. ❖❖❖

5
Selection of Gem Stones According to the Stars

You can choose your suitable gem according to your star also. In all, there are 27 stars. Each star is ruled by a specific planet. First you should know your star. Then you should find out which planet is the ruler of that star. Only then you can know about the gem of that planet and choose it to wear.

1. **Ashwini:** The ruler of this star is Ketu, the gem of Ketu is Cat's Eye. If one wears Cat's Eye, it would cure different types of diseases and make one healthy and wealthy. He would be attracted by others.

2. **Bharani:** The ruler of this star is Venus. The gem of Venus is Diamond. Persons born in Bharani star can wear Diamond. Use of Diamond brings material prosperity and happiness.

3. **Krittika:** The ruler of this star is the Sun. The gem of the Sun is Ruby. Persons born in Krittika star can wear Ruby. Its use produces good health, success in finance and helps to win over enemies.

4. **Rohini:** The ruler of this star is Moon. The gem of Moon is White Pearl. Persons born under Rohini star can wear Pearl as their lucky gem. It brings position, wealth and success in life.

5. **Mrigashira:** The ruler of this star is Mars. The gem of Mars is Coral. So persons born under Mrigashira can wear Coral as their lucky gem. Wearing of Red Coral brings peace of mind, purity of heart, boldness and also helps in controlling anger and wild passions.

6. **Ardra:** The ruler of this star is Rahu. Its gem is Gomeda. So persons born under this star can wear Gomeda for seeking fortune. It also bestows intelligence, fame, success in all ventures and peace of mind and self-confidence. The subject would overcome selfishness.

7. **Punarvasu:** The lord of this star is Guru (Jupiter). The gem that should be worn by persons born under this star is Yellow Sapphire (Pukhraj). It brings good luck. It also gives success, fulfilment of desires, healthy body and mind—and makes one rich.

8. **Pushyami:** The lord of this star is Saturn, and the gem is Blue Sapphire. Persons born under Pushya star can wear Blue Sapphire as their birth stone and get success. It enables them to get money, riches, prosperity, fame, name, house, property, conveyance and luxuries. Moreover, it gives them peace of mind and spiritual inclination.

9. **Ashlesha:** The lord of this star is Mercury. Its gem is Emerald. Persons born under this star should wear Emerald to get success. They will get good rewards for their talent. Emerland

washes away their sins. It can bestow happiness and fortune on them.

10. **Makha:** The owner of this star is Ketu. Its gem is Cat's Eye. Persons born under Makha should wear Cat's Eye as their birth stone to get success in life. By wearing Cat's Eye, they can get name, fame and popularity. It can make them spiritual. It will make them calm and God fearing.

11. **Purva Phalguni:** Its Lord is Shukra, i.e., Venus. So, persons born under this star, should wear Diamond for success. It can give them status, good family life, luxuries and property. They would get multiple profits through business. It will give them charm and beauty.

12. **Uttara Phalguni:** Its owner is Surya, the Sun. The gem for this star is Ruby. Persons born under Uttara Phalguni can wear Ruby for good luck. It will bestow upon them health, wealth, happiness, good status, success and majestic attraction.

13. **Hasta:** The owner of this star is Moon. Its gem is White Pearl. So Hasta-born persons should wear White Pearl as their lucky gem. By wearing Pearl, they can get peace of mind, creativity, longevity, good health, success, wealth, riches, name, fame and also popularity.

14. **Chitra:** The Lord of Chitra is Mars. Its gem is Coral. So Chitra-born persons should wear Red Coral for good luck. It enables them to have good health, wisdom, spirituality, success, position and also domestic harmony.

15. **Swati:** The Lord of Swati is Rahu. Its gem is Gomeda. Swati-born persons should wear Gomeda. It can bring them growth in their business or profession. It can ward off any adverse effect of evil eye and black magic. It can make a person active and provide him with high position, name, fame and wealth.

16. **Vishakha:** Its Lord is Guru (Jupiter). Its gem is the Yellow Sapphire. Vishakha-born persons should wear Yellow Sapphire for good luck. It would bestow royal honour, prestige and health.

17. **Anuradha:** Its lord is Saturn. Its gem is the Blue Sapphire. So Anuradha-born persons should wear Blue Sapphire for a happy life. It bestows happiness, prosperity and also wisdom.

18. **Jyeshta:** The ruler of this star is Mercury. The gem of Mercury is Emerald. So Jyeshta-born persons should wear Emerald as their lucky gem. It would help them improve their behaviour and conduct. Their anger would cool down, and they will enjoy a happy life.

19. **Moola:** The ruler of this star is Ketu. The gem of Ketu is Cat's Eye. Moola-born persons should wear Cat's Eye as their lucky gem. It will give them calm and peaceful mind. They will receive help from relatives and friends and win over enemies.

20. **Purvashada:** The ruler of this star is Venus. The gem of Venus is Diamond. Purvashada-born persons should wear Diamond as their lucky gem. By wearing Diamond, they will get wealth, comfort, house, vehicle, landed property etc.

21. **Uttarashada:** The owner of this star is the Sun.

The gem of Sun is Ruby. Hence, Uttarashada-born persons should wear Ruby as their lucky gem. It brings wealth and prosperous life.

22. **Shravana:** The owner of this star is Moon. The gem of Moon is Pearl. Persons born under this star should wear White Pearl. They will have a fulfilling life, and their position would improve.

23. **Dhanishta:** The ruler of this star is Mars. The gem of Mars is Red Coral. So Dhanishta-born persons should wear Red Coral as their lucky gem. It brings success in all ventures. They rise in profession. It protects them from dangers and accidents.

24. **Shatabhisha:** The owner of this star is Rahu. The gem of Rahu is Gomeda. So Shatabhisha-born persons should wear Gomeda as their lucky gem. It ensures success in life, good health, and a happy life and gives strength to win over estranged relatives.

25. **Purvabhadra:** The owner of this star is Jupiter. The gem of Jupiter is Yellow Sapphire. So Purvabhadra-born persons should wear Yellow Sapphire as their lucky gem. This would restore them their lost prosperity, children's welfare, promotion in service, professional success and happiness.

26. **Uttarabhadra:** The owner of this star is Saturn. The gem of Saturn is Blue Sapphire. So Uttarabhadra-born persons should wear Blue Sapphire as their lucky gem. It brings success in the profession or business, acquisition of building and landed property, name, fame and respect in society.

27. **Revati:** The owner of this star is Mercury. The

gem of Mercury is Emerald. Hence, Revati-born persons should wear Emerald as their lucky gem. Emerald brings comforts in life. It would also help them acquire property and success in their profession.

6

Selection of Gem According to Numerology

Although one may select one's lucky gem according to one's Zodiac sign or the Star; selecting the same through numerology is the best way. As planets work on numbers so powerfully, the numerological way of selecting the gem is regarded as perfect and more rewarding than selecting the same through other methods. To know the number of a particular person, different methods have been discussed in chapter 7.

The Method of Selecting the Gem through Numerological Method

Ashwini: If we go by the ruling Star, the gem for Ashwini-born persons is Cat's Eye. According to the Rashi, it is the Red Coral. But choosing the numerological way is the best one. Ashwini-born persons with 1, 3, 9 numbers should wear Red Coral, Ashwini born persons with 2, 5, 6, 7, 8 numbers should wear Cat's Eye to get maximum benefits, and those with number 4 can avoid both and opt for Gomeda.

Bharani: According to the Star, the gem is Diamond. According to the Rashi, it is Red Coral. So Bharani-born persons in 1, 3, 9 numbers should wear Red Coral, and those with 2, 4, 5, 6, 7, 8 numbers should wear Diamond to get maximum benefits.

Krithika: According to the Star, the gem is Ruby. According to the Rashi, the gem is Red Coral. Krithika-born persons in 1, 3, 9, 6 numbers should wear Red Coral. But those with 2, 4, 5, 7 numbers can wear Ruby to get the benefits. But number 8 should avoid both, and opt for Aquamarine.

Rohini: According to the ruling Star, the gem is White Pearl. According to the Rashi, it is Diamond. Rohini-born persons in 1, 9, 2, 4, 7 numbers should wear White Pearl, and those with 5, 6, 8 numbers should wear Diamond, while '3' born should avoid both and wear Topaz to get benefits.

Mrigashira: According to the Star, the gem is Red Coral. According to the Rashi, it is Diamond and Emerald. Mrigashira-born persons in 2, 4, 5, 6, 8, 7 numbers should wear Diamond and in 1, 3, 9 numbers, they should wear Red Coral.

Ardra: According to the Star, the gem is Gomeda. According to the Rashi, it is Emerald. Ardra-born persons in 1, 2, 4, 5, 6 numbers can wear Gomeda. While 1, 2, 4, 5, 6, 8, 7 numbers can wear Emerald, 3 and 9 should avoid both and wear their Birth Stone instead.

Punarvasu: While according to the Star, the gem is Yellow Sapphire, according to the Rashi, it is Emerald. Punarvasu-born persons in 1, 3, 9 numbers can wear Yellow Sapphire, while those in 2, 4, 5, 6, 7, 8 numbers should wear Emerald to get maximum benefits.

Pushya: According to the Star, the gem is Blue Sapphire. According to the Rashi, it is White Pearl. Pushya-born persons in 1, 2, 4, 7, 9 numbers should wear Pearl. Those with 5, 6, 8 numbers should wear Blue Sapphire, to get benefits. '3' born should avoid both, and wear their Birth Stone.

Aslesha: According to the Star, it is Emerald. According to the Rashi, it is White Pearl. Aslesha-born persons in 1, 2, 7, 9 numbers should wear Pearl and 4, 5, 6, 8 number-born should wear Emerald to get benefits. The '3' should avoid both, and wear Birth Stone.

Makha: According to the Star, the gem is Cat's Eye. According to the Rashi, it is Ruby. Makha-born persons in 1, 3, 4, 9 numbers should wear Ruby as their lucky gem. And 2, 5, 6, 7, 8 numbers should wear Cat's Eye to get maximum benefits.

Purva Phalguni: According to the Star, the gem is Diamond. According to the Rashi, it is Ruby. Purva Phalguni-born persons in 1, 3, 9 numbers should wear Ruby as their lucky gem. Those with 2, 4, 5, 6, 7, 8, 9 numbers should wear Diamond to get maximum benefits.

Uttara Phalguni: According to the Star, the gem is Ruby. According to the Rashi, also it is Ruby. So the Uttara Phalguni-born should wear Ruby-while '8' and '6' born should avoid Ruby, and should wear their Birth Stone.

Hasta: According to the Star, the gem is Pearl, according to the Rashi, it is Emerald. Persons born on 2, 7, 9 can wear Pearl while persons born on 1, 4, 5, 6, 7, 8 can wear Emerald. The number '3' born person should avoid both and wear their Birth Stone.

Chitra: According to the Star, the Gem for Chitra is Coral. But according to the Rashi, it is Emerald/Diamond. The 1, 3, 9 born Chitra can wear Red Coral while 2, 4, 5, 6, 7, 8 born Chitra can wear Emerald/Diamond for getting success.

Swati: According to the Star, the gem is Gomeda. According to the Rashi, it is Diamond. The 1, 4 born can wear Gomeda for good luck while 2, 5, 6, 7, 8, 9 can wear Diamond for success. The '3' born should avoid both, and wear Birth Stone.

Vishakha: According to the Star, the gem is Yellow Sapphire, but according to the Rashi, it is Diamond. The 1, 3, 9 born persons can wear Yellow Sapphire, or Coral. while the 2, 4, 5, 6, 7, 8 born persons can wear Diamond for maximum benefit.

Anuradha: According to the Star, the gem is Blue Sapphire, but according to the Rashi, it is Red Coral. So persons born on 1, 3, 9 can wear Red Coral and persons born on 5, 6, 7, 8 can wear blue sapphire. The 2 and 4 born persons should avoid both, and wear their Birth Stone.

Jyeshta: According to the Star, the gem is Emerald. According to the Rashi, it is Red Coral. So persons born on 1, 3, 9 can wear Red Coral, whereas 2, 4, 5, 6, 7, 8 born persons can wear Emerald for maximum benefit.

Moola: According to the Star, the gem is Cat's Eye. According to the Rashi, it is Yellow Sapphire. Persons born on 1, 3, 9 can wear Yellow Sapphire. Persons born on 2, 5, 6, 7, 8 can wear Cat's Eye for health, wealth and prosperity. The number '4' should avoid both, and wear Gomeda.

Purvashada: According to the Star, the gem is Diamond. According to the Rashi, it is Yellow

Sapphire. Persons born on 1, 3, 9 can wear Yellow Sapphire and persons born on 2, 4, 5, 6, 7, 8 can wear Diamond for better luck.

Uttarashada: According to the Star, the gem is Ruby but according to the Rashi, it is Blue Sapphire. Persons born on 1, 3, 4, 9 can wear Ruby whereas persons born on 2, 5, 6, 7, 8 can wear Blue Sapphire for prosperity and success.

Shravana: According to the Star, the gem is White Pearl. But according to the Rashi, it is Blue Sapphire. Persons born on 1, 2, 4, 9 can wear White Pearl, whereas persons born on 3, 5, 6, 7, 8 can wear Blue Sapphire to get maximum benefits.

Dhanishta: According to the Star, the gem is Red Coral and according to the Rashi, it is Blue Sapphire. Persons born on 1, 3, 9 can wear Red Coral while those with 5, 6, 7, 8 numbers can wear Blue Sapphire. The numbers 2 and 4 should avoid both, and wear their Birth Stone.

Shatabhisha: According to the Star, the gem is Gomeda, but according to the Rashi, it is Blue Sapphire. So persons born on 1, 2, 4 can wear Gomeda and persons born on 5, 6, 7, 8 can wear Blue Sapphire. The '3', '9' born should avoid both, and choose their Birth Stones.

Purvabhadra: According to the Star, the gem is Yellow Sapphire, but according to the Rashi, it is Blue Sapphire. So persons born on 1, 3, 9 can wear Yellow Sapphire. Persons born on 5, 6, 7, 8 can wear Blue Sapphire and persons born on 2 and 4 should avoid both, and wear their Birth Stone.

Uttarabhadra: According to the Star, the gem is Blue Sapphire and according to the Rashi, it is Yellow Sapphire. Persons born on 1, 3, 9 can wear

Yellow Sapphire, whereas persons born on 5, 6, 7, 8 can wear Blue Sapphire. However, persons born on 2 and 4 should avoid both, and wear their Birth Stones.

Revati: According to the Star, the gem is Emerald. According to the Rashi, it is Yellow Sapphire. Persons born on 2, 4, 5, 6, 7, 8 can wear Emerald and persons born on 1, 3, 9 dates can wear Yellow Sapphire for health, wealth and prosperity.

7
Gems and Numerology

Gems can also be selected on the basis of Numerology. There are three ways of selecting gems through Numerology.

1. Based on the date of birth.
2. Based on the total value of name number.
3. Based on the month of birth.

I. Let us discuss about the ways in which a lucky gem is selected on the basis of date of birth.

1. Persons born on **1, 10, 19, 28** of all months are ruled by the Sun (Surya). So they can wear Ruby, Star Ruby, Garnet, Peridot, Golden Topaz, Amber and get success in all ventures.

2. Persons born on **2, 11, 20, 29** of all months are ruled by Moon. They can wear Pearl, Moonstone, Jade and get success, mental peace, co-operation of others and a steady mind. They would get good sleep and improved circulation of blood.

3. Persons born on **3, 12, 21, 30** of all months can wear Yellow Sapphire, Yellow Topaz, Yellow Tourmaline to get success in family life and social contacts. It brings intelligence,

opportunities, popularity and material comforts in domestic life. It reduces disorders of chest and lungs.

4. Persons born on **4, 13, 22, 31** of all months can wear Gomeda, Hessonite Garnet, Jaichint to get organisational power, discipline, justice, activity, energy, financial stability and gradual progress in life. It reduces the diseases of feet, knees and all types of urinary problems.

5. Persons born on **5, 14, 23** of all months can wear Emerald, Aquamarine, Green Tourmaline, Green Onyx, Malachite to be blessed with writing skill, happiness, stability in finance, gains in business, speculation and travel. It makes them talented, improves their diplomatic skills and eloquence. It helps in curing or controlling ailments related to liver, lungs and nerves.

6. Persons born on **6, 15, 24** of all months can wear Turquoise, Diamond, Spathic, White Tourmaline to get good education, material prosperity, quick marriage and harmony at home. It gives harmony, beauty and rhythm. It also ensures co-operation and sympathy from others. One would be adored by one and all.

7. Persons born on **7, 16, 25** of all months can wear Cat's Eye/Tiger Eye to get success, good health, wealth and spiritual upliftment. It also helps music composers, actors, inventors, scientists and research scholars in their professions. It brings orginality and an independent nature. It also reduces health problems such as nervousness, fever, boils etc.

8. Persons born on **8, 17, 26** of all months can wear Blue Sapphire, Blue Tourmaline, Star Sapphire, Lolite/Lapis Lazuli to get good health, energy, luck, wealth, multiple profits and cultural development. It reduces the problems of ears, joints and teeth. It removes delays, poverty and obstacles.

9. Persons born on **9, 18, 27** of all months can wear Red Coral/Red Jasper/Red Tourmaline to get success, healing, strength and boldness. It keeps one's temper in check and gives courage and resistance. One would lead a happy family life, and achieve wealth. It reduces the problem of kidney, piles and fever.

II. According to Numerology each letter has a value. If the total value is added it forms a single digit. Stones can also be selected on the basis of this single digit.

How to Calculate

First let us know the value of each letter.

A, I, J, Y, Q = 1   E, H, N, X = 5

B, R, K   = 2   U, V, W   = 6

C, S, L, G   = 3   O, Z   = 7

D, T, M   = 4   F, P   = 8

Now suppose the name of a person is N. AJAY KUMAR. It should be added with the method as given hereunder.

N + A J A Y K U M A R
5 + 1 + 1 + 1 + 1 + 2 + 6 + 4 + 1 + 2 i.e., 24
= 2 + 4 = 6

So you should wear stone for '6' number.

If the name is Amoolya Bajaj.

them A M O O L Y A + B A J A J

1 + 4 + 7 + 7 + 3 + 1 + 1   2 + 1 + 1 + 1 + 1   = 30 = 3 + 0 = 3

So the stone for '3' should be worn.

The lucky gems for all the numbers have been given earlier in the chapter.

III. Selection of Gem Based on Month of Birth

1. Persons born between **15th January** and **15th February** are ruled by Saturn. So they can wear Blue Sapphire/Emerald to get luck, happiness and financial stability. Health problems related to bile, joint pain, nervousness would be overcome.

2. Persons born between **15th February** and **15th March** are ruled by Saturn. So they can wear Blue Sapphire, Amethyst, Lapis Lazuli to get honour, prestige and riches. These help in all types of kidney problems.

3. Persons born between **15th March** and **15th April** are ruled by Jupiter. So, they can wear Yellow Sapphire, Amethyst, Golden Topaz/Yellow Topaz. These would give them courage, success, generosity and control over fickle mind. These help in controlling insomnia.

4. Persons born between **15th April** and **15th May** are ruled by Mars. So they can wear Red Coral/Garnet/Red Jasper/Bloodstone/Red Tourmaline. These would give them dominance, energy, luck. These also help in reducing the problems of eyes, ears, teeth and inflammation.

5. Persons born between **15th May** and **15th June** are ruled by Venus. So they can wear

Diamond/Turquoise/White Zircon or Spathik. These will give them all kinds of luxuries, prosperity, generosity and endurance. These will help in reducing respiratory problems.

6. Persons born between **15th June** and **15th July** are ruled by Mercury. So they can wear Emerald, Aquamarine, Green Tourmaline, Onyx or Malachite. These will give them brilliance, profit in business and luck. These reduce psychological problems.

7. Persons born between **15th July** and **15th August** are ruled by Moon. So they can wear Pearl, Moonstone or Jade. By wearing these gems, they can advance in the industry. These give success in arts, speculation and occupation. These reduce gastric problems.

8. Persons born between **15th August** and **15th September** are ruled by Sun. They can wear Ruby/Golden Topaz/Amber. These will give them dignity, success in bringing out talent, favour from government and good financial status. These reduce the feeling of fatigue.

9. Persons born between **15th September** and **15th October** are ruled by Mercury. They can wear Emerald, Green Tourmaline or Aquamarine. These bestow oratorial skills, enhanced profits and steady growth. These also reduce the problem of nervousness.

10. Persons born between **15th October** and **15th November** are ruled by Venus. They can wear Diamond, Turquoise or Spathic. These will give them charm, enthusiasm, energy and luxurious life. These reduce the impurities of skin and blood.

11. Persons born between **15th November** and **15th December** are ruled by Mars. So they can wear Red Coral, Red Jasper or Cornelian. These bestow courage, energy, property and luck. These reduce throat problems.

12. Persons born between **15th December** and **15th January** are ruled by Jupiter. So they can wear Yellow Sapphire/Yellow Jasper or Yellow Tourmaline etc. These will bring enhanced financial status, health and spiritual upliftment and also reduce joint pains.

8
Selection of Gems Based on First Letter of the Name

Some people do not know their correct date of birth. Such persons can choose the lucky gem based on the first letter of their name.

The first letter of the name denotes a star. Based on this star, they have to select the lucky gem.

1. **SU, CHE, CHO, LA:** According to these letters, the star is Ashwini and the gem is Cat's Eye or Tiger Eye. By wearing Cat's Eye, they can get position, financial stability, happiness, multiple profits, magnetic personality, success in education, research etc.

2. **LI, LU, LE, LO:** According to these letters, the star is Bharani and the gem is Diamond/ Turquoise. By wearing a Diamond or Turquoise, one can get promotion, luxuries, intelligence, happy married life, children, conveyance and property.

3. **A, E, U, Y:** According to these letters, the star is Krittika and the gem is Ruby, Star Ruby or Garnet. These can bestow success in all ventures, good support from friends, relatives

and superiors. One would also get rise in one's financial position and come out of legal problems.

4. **O, VA, VI, VU:** According to these letters, the star is Rohini and the gem is Pearl, Moonstone or Jade. By wearing it one can get lost property, enemies can become friends. These would also bring name, fame and popularity.

5. **VE, VO, KA, KI:** According to these letters, the star is Mrigashira and the gem is Red Coral, Red Cornelian or Red Tourmaline. By wearing these, one can get oratorial skill, prosperity, boldness and firmness in decisions. These also protect one from all sorts of accidents and weapons.

6. **KU, KA, JA, CHA:** According to these letters, the star is Ardra and the gem is Gomeda/Hessonite Garnet or Jaichint. By wearing these, one can get a clear mind and progress. One would come out of bad company, bad habits and get control over short temper. Success is ensured in occupation.

7. **KE, KO, HA, HI:** According to these letters, the star is Punarvasu and the gem is Yellow Sapphire, Golden Topaz, Yellow Topaz or Amethyst. By wearing these, one can obtain intelligence, good health, position, happy family life, God's grace and support from all sides.

8. **HU, HI, HO, D:** These letters belong to the star Pushyami. Its gems are Blue Sapphire, Amethyst/Lapis Lazuli, Lolit/Blue Tourmaline or Star Sapphire. Through these, one can get attraction, property, good character and position. Health problems connected to 'vata'

get reduced. Obstacles and disappointments also get reduced.

9. **DI, DO, DE, DU:** These letters belong to the star Aslesha. Its gems are Emerald, Aquamarine, Green Tourmaline, Green Onyx and Malachite. By wearing these, one can get mental peace, good education, happiness and success. Health problems and nervousness will be reduced. Intelligence, name and fame will be achieved.

10. **MA, MI, MU, ME:** These letters belong to Makha. Its gems are Cat's Eye and Tiger Eye. By wearing these, one can get wealth, luxuries, God's grace, happy life, intelligence, property and success in all ventures. These make a person spiritual.

11. **MO, TA, TI, TU:** These letters belong to the star Purva Phalguni. Its gems are Diamond, Turquoise, Spathic, White Tourmaline, Zircon. By wearing these, one can get oratorial skill, luxuries, attraction, quick marriage, progress in life and boldness. Life will be full of happiness.

12. **TE, TO, PA, PI:** These letters belong to the star Uttara Phalguni. The gems are Ruby, Star Ruby, Garnet, Peridot, Golden Topaz. By wearing these, one can achieve magnetic and charming personality, friends and support from superiors. These help in abundant flow of money, luxuries and attainment of property.

13. **POO, SHA, NO, TA:** These letters belong to the star Hasta. Its gems are Moon Stone, Pearl or Jade. By wearing these, one can achieve mental peace, good health, longevity and affection from family members. One comes out

of all kinds of lung problems. These also bring strong mind, status and abundant money.

14. **PE, PO, TA, R:** These letters belong to the star Chitra. Its gems are Red Coral, Red Jasper, Cornelian or Red Tourmaline. By wearing these, one can achieve success in legal cases, job, marriage, money, jewellery, and success in business. These will protect you from dangers related to fire and electricity.

15. **RU, RA, RO, HA:** These letters belong to the star Swati. Its gems are Gomeda/Hessonite, Garnet and Jaichint. By wearing these, one can achieve success in legal cases and come out of illegal matters, if any. These also bestow good health and status. These remove obstacles and disappointments. These also make one rich and prosperous.

16. **THI, TH, THE, THO:** These letters belong to the star Vishakha. Its gems are Yellow Sapphire, Amethyst, Yellow Zircon, Yellow Tourmaline, Yellow Topaz. By putting on these gems, Vishakha-born can achieve God's grace, children, good wife, property, intelligence and happiness.

17. **NE, NI, NO, NE:** These letters belong to the star Anuradha. Its gems are Blue Sapphire, Lapiz Lasuli, Blue Zircon, Blue Tourmaline or Star Sapphire. By wearing any of these, one can get the power of magnetic attraction, progress in life and success. These also ensure peace of mind and quick success in all ventures.

18. **YO, YA, YI, YU:** The star of these letters is Jyeshta. Its gems are Emerald/Aquamarine/ Green Onyx/Green Tourmaline, Green Jade etc. These bring success, happiness, skill to make

decisions and implement them. These also help in controlling all types of nervous problems.

19. **YE, YO, BA, BI:** These letters belong to the Moola star. Its gem is Cat's Eye or Tiger Eye. Through this, one can achieve property and ward off the evil spirits and bad company etc. It will make one spiritual and help him get rid of all types of chronic diseases. It also ensures financial position.

20. **BOO, DHA, BHA, DA:** These letters belong to the star Purvashada. Its gems are Diamond, Spathic, Turquoise, White Tourmaline or American Diamond. By wearing these, one can get house, conveyance, jewels, property, happy married life, children, success and luxuries. If these are worn by a businessman, he will achieve multiple profits. These also help in bringing people out of diseases.

21. **BE, BO, JHA, JI:** These letters belong to Uttarashada. Its gems are Ruby, Star Ruby, Peridot, Golden Topaz, or Garnet. By wearing Ruby, one can get support from superiors, friends and relatives. One would get favours from the Government. They would also get all types of happiness, property, good conduct and magnetic attraction.

22. **JU, JE, JO, KHAA:** These letters belong to the star Shravana. Its gems are White Pearl, Jade or Moon Stone. By wearing these, one can achieve mental peace, and lot of wealth. These will make one bold and ensure help and support of the opposite sex. These also bring a luxurious life.

23. **GA, GI, GU, GE:** According to these letters, the star is Dhanishta and its gems are Red Coral,

Red Tourmaline, Red Jasper or Red Cornelian. These can help one get over short temper and become calm. These give physical and mental strength, landed property, name, fame and wealth.

24. **GO, SA, SI, SU:** According to these letters, the star is Shatabhisha and the gems are Gomeda, Hessonite Garnet or Jaichint. By wearing these stones, one can get success in legal, property cases. These also help the subjects to come out of all subjugation and lead a happy life. They would come out of all bad habits. Health, wealth, happiness and respect from others would be ensured.

25. **SE, SO, DHA, DHI:** According to these letters, the star is Purvabhadra and the gems are Yellow Sapphire, Yellow Tourmaline, Yellow Topaz, Golden Topaz, Yellow Jasper and Yellow Cornelian. These can bestow God's grace, good children and spouse. One would get landed property, charm and financial stability.

26. **DHE, SYAM, CH, DHA:** These letters belong to the star Uttarashada. Its gems are Blue Sapphire, Blue Tourmaline, Lapis Lazuli, Lolit, Blue Zircon, Blue Topaz and Star Sapphire. These bring name and fame and help in removing obstacles and disappointments. One would get good servants, subordinates, property and good health.

27. **DHE, DHO, CHA, CHI:** These letters belong to the star Revati. Its gems are Emerald, Aquamarine, Green Onyx, Green Tourmaline and Green Jade. By wearing these, one can get intelligence, wisdom, children, financial stability, good reputation, literary skills and happiness.

❖❖❖

9
Pooja for Stones
Precious and Semi-precious Gems

Any person who desires to wear a stone, whether a precious or a semi-precious one, should do so on a prescribed day after performing the necessary rituals for the stone. By doing such rituals, we are awakening the power of the planet which vests in it. By doing so, we can make it give off its vibrations or emanations from its material body in a faster manner. Pooja for Navaratanas has been held in great esteem. Each stone carries in itself the planetary attraction of a particular planet. As a result, the rituals should be observed on the particular planet's day for maximum benefit. It will strengthen its influence. The day and time for each stone are discussed in detail in the following pages. By performing the rituals, we can attract the favour and grace of the said planet. Metals also play a very important role in this respect. Metals are also deeply related to the planets and stars; so the correct choice makes a lot of difference. This relation between the metals and gems is enduring and unchangeable.

NO.	PLANETS	METALS
1.	Sun	Copper or Gold
2.	Moon	Silver
3.	Jupiter	Gold
4.	Rahu	Copper or Silver
5.	Mercury	Silver or Brass
6.	Venus	Silver
7.	Ketu	Silver
8.	Saturn	Silver
9.	Mars	Gold or Copper

After the stone is set in the right combination of gems and metals, it acquires added power through the rituals and then it can be worn at the appropriate hour.

Method of Pooja for Wearing Gem Stones

1. RUBY

Pooja should be done on any Sunday during "Marshora" between 5am and 6am or 12 noon and 1pm.

Necessary Pooja Articles

1. Red Silk Cloth, 2. Wheat, 3. Dhoop Sticks, 4. Lamp, 5. 21 Yellow Flowers, and 6. Prasad of Wheat-Rawa Upma.

Method

Spread red silk cloth before God's idol and put wheat on it. First wash the ring with the stone set in it. Then apply Sandal, Kumkum on it and place it on the red silk cloth.

Now light the lamps with 5 faces i.e., (5 wicks). Burn dhoop stick, and perform pooja to the ring with yellow flowers reciting Surya Mantra. Offer Upma as Prasad. Now wear the ring. After the ring is worn, donate jaggery to get maximum benefit.

Surya Mantra

Ashwa Dwajaaya Vidhmahe
Paasha Hasthaaya Dheemahi
Tanno Surya Prachodayath

Recite this mantra 108 times. (After the Pooja is over, divide the yellow flowers into 5 parts, distribute among the family members).

2. PEARL

Pooja should be done on Monday during "Chandra Hora" i.e., between 6am and 7am or 8pm and 9pm.

Necessary Pooja Articles

1. One plate, 2. One kalash, 3. Rice, 4. Curd, 5. Jasmine flowers, 6. Shiv-Parvati photo.

Method

Pour curd in the kalash and put the Pearl ring in it. Apply sandal, turmeric and kumkum to the kalash. Take a plate and spread rice on it. Now place the kalash on this plate. Close the kalash with another plate and then place Shiv-Parvati photo on it. Perform archana to Parvati Devi with Jasmine flowers. After the archana is complete, take rice and perform archana to Moon on the rice plate. Offer "**Milk Kheer**" as Prasad. After wearing the Pearl ring, donate milk and **mishri**.

Moon Mantra

> *Padma Dwajaaya Vidhmahe*
> *Hema Roopaya Dheemahi*
> *Tanno Soma Prachodayath*

Parvati Mantra

> *Amba Saambavi Chandramouli Rabalaam Aparna Uma Parvati, Kaali, Haimavati, Siva Trinayanaa, Kaathyaayini Bhairavi.*

3. EMERALD

Pooja should be done on Wednesday during the "Budha Hora" i.e., 6-7am or 1-2pm

Necessary Pooja Articles

1. One Plate, 2. One Kalash made of Silver or Steel, 3. Rice, 4. Sandal, Kumkum, 5 Betel leaves (five), 6. Coconut, 7. Green Cloth, 8. Flower Garland, 9. Milk, Sugar, Saffron, Mishri, Elaichi, Eatable Camphor and Rose Water, 10. Any sweet for Prasad.

Method

Take a plate and spread rice over it. Take the kalash and apply Chandan–3 lines each, five times consecutively. Apply Kumkum.

Now, place the kalash over rice plate, pour milk into the kalash mixed with sugar, saffron, mishri, elaichi, eatable camphor and eatable rose water. Now put the Emerald ring in the milk. Keep 5 betel leaves on the kalash. On it, keep coconut and apply sandal, kumkum to the coconut. Put green cloth, flower garland, and perform Lakshmi Mantra 324 times i.e., 108 times thrice. Offer sweet as Prasad. After the pooja, wear the Emerald Ring. After wearing the Emerald, donate green gram.

Lakshmi Mantra

Maha Devaicha Vidhmahe
Vishnu Patnaicha Dheemahi
Tanno Lakshmi Prachodayath

4. RED CORAL

Pooja should be done on Tuesday, Thursday and Sunday for 9 days during "Mars Hora" i.e.,

Tuesday : 6-7am or 1-2pm
Thursday : 7-8am or 2-3pm
Sunday : 5-6am or 12-1pm

Necessary Pooja Articles

1. Red Silk Clothes (two), 2. Copper plate, 3. Tuar Dal, 4. Red Flowers, 5. Raagi, 6. Honey.

Method

Place the red silk clothes before God and spread tuar dal on it. Place the copper plate over the dal. Now place another red silk on it and again spread tuar dal on it. Wash the Coral ring, apply sandal and kumkum. Take 3, 6 or 9 red flowers, tie them to the ring with the help of a red thread and place the ring on tuar dal.

Begin the pooja on one Tuesday and perform continuously for 9 times i.e., on Tuesdays, Thursdays and Sundays. On the 9th day, wear the ring after pooja. During the pooja days, after the pooja, tie the Red Coral in a red silk cloth and keep it. Offer honey as Prasad, recite Mars Mantra and perform pooja with raagi. After pooja is complete, donate masoor dal in a red cover.

Mars Mantra

Veera Dwajaaya Vidhmahe
Vigna Hastaaya Dheemahi
Tanno Bhowma Prachodayath

5. DIAMOND

Pooja should be done on Friday during the "Shukra Hora" i.e., 6-7am or 1-2pm.

Necessary Pooja Articles

1. One triangular-shaped plate, 2. Blue silk cloth cut into a triangular piece, 3. Rajma, 4. Sandal, Kumkum, 5. 5 types of flowers, 5 types of fruits and 5 types of sweets, 6. 30 betel leaves, 5 blouse pieces, 7. Camphor, 8. 5 packets of betel nuts, 9. Haldi pieces.

Method

Take one steel plate of triangular shape and spread Rajma over it. On this, put blue silk cloth in triangular shape. On this blue silk cloth, keep the Diamond ring after applying sandal and kumkum to it. Now recite Lakshmi Mantra 108 times and after that, Shukra Mantra 108 times. Repeat this process for 5 times, i.e., 5 times 108 Lakshmi Mantra and 5 times 108 Shukra Mantra. Recite this mantra with 5 types of flowers. After completing the ritual, offer 5 types of sweets and 5 types of fruits. Put on the ring. Now distribute betel leaves, haldi pieces, betel nuts, flowers, fruits, sweets and blouse pieces to five ladies and complete the pooja.

Lakshmi Mantra

Maha Devaicha Vidhmahe
Vishnu Patnaicha Dheemahi
Tanno Lakshmi Prachodayath

Shukra Mantra

Ashwa Dwajaaya Vidhmahe,
Dhanur Hasthaaya Dheemahi
Tanno Shukra Prachodayath

6. PUSHYARAGA (Yellow Sapphire)

Pooja should be performed on any Thursday during the "Hora of Guru" i.e., 6-7am or 1-2pm.

Necessary Pooja Articles

1. Yellow coloured cloth (Mango Colour), 2. Bengal Gram (Coated), 3. Sandal, Kumkum, 4. Ketaki flowers or Marigold flowers, 5. Prasad i.e., Kheer made of Jaggery and Moong Dal.

Method

Spread the yellow cloth before God. Spread Bengal gram over it. On the dal, apply sandal, kumkum to the ring and place it on the dal. Take 3 ketaki flowers, or 3 marigold flowers and recite Lalita Sahasnanama. After reciting, take the Bengal gram dal, and do Guru Mantra 108 times. After pooja, offer kheer made of moong dal and jaggery. After wearing the ring donate Bengal gram.

Guru Mantra

Vrishabha Dwajaaya Vidhmahe
Gruni Hasthaaya Dheemahi
Tanno Guruh Prachodayath

7. NEELAM (Blue Sapphire)

Pooja should be performed on any Saturday between 6-7am or 1-2pm in the afternoon.

Necessary Pooja Articles

1. Iron or Steel Plate-1, 2. Steel Lamp-1, 3. Black til, 4. Sandal, Kumkum, 5. Blue flowers, 6. Eight pieces black cloth.

Method

Keep the iron or steel plate. Light the steel lamp. Spread til over the plate. Wash the ring, apply sandal and kumkum to it and place it on the plate. Recite

Shani Mantra for 108 times with blue flowers. Offer Prasad of til rice (cooked rice mixed with til). Offer this til rice, black cloth (if it is winter, donate black shawl) to eight beggars or poor people alongwith Rs. 10/- to each one. After pooja is over, take the ring to Ayyappa Temple. Perform the pooja there and wear it.

Shani Mantra

Kaka Dwajaaya Vidhmahe
Kadga Hasthaaya Dheemahi
Tanno Mandha Prachodayath

8. GOMEDA

Pooja should be performed on any Wednesday between 6am and 7am or 1pm and 2pm.

Necessary Pooja Articles

1. One snake idol, 2. Pieces of brown clothes, 3. Kg. of black urad dal, 4. Sandal, Kumkum, 5. 22 coins of same denomination, 6. 16 flowers, 7. Yellow rice, 8. Prasad made of milk and plantain.

Method

Place the snake idol in front. Spread brown cloth around it. Spread 1/2 kg. black urad dal over it, and again spread brown cloth over it. Then again spread urad dal over it. Wash Gomeda and apply sandal, kumkum to it. Take one flower and tie it with the ring with a red thread. Now place the Gomeda ring over the black urad dal. Now place all around it 22 coins and 16 flowers. Now take yellow rice and perform 108 times the Rahu Mantra. After pooja, offer plantain mixed with milk. After pooja is over, cut the brown cloth into 17 pieces. On every piece, place one part of urad dal. Place one coin in it, and tie them into 17 bundles and donate to 17 beggars. Now put the remaining 5 coins in your cash box.

Rahu Mantra

> *Naaga Dwajaaya Vidhmahe*
> *Padma Hasthaaya Dheemahi*
> *Tanno Rahu Prachodayath*

9. CAT'S EYE

Pooja should be performed on Wednesday between 6am and 7am to 1pm and 2pm or between 8pm and 9pm.

Necessary Pooja Articles

1. One snake idol, 2. One brass plate, 3. Grey or red cloth, 4. Horse gram, 5. Sandal, Kumkum, 6. Curd for offering, 7. One small bowl of sugar.

Method

Place the snake idol in front. Inside or before it, place the brass plate and spread grey or red cloth over the brass plate. Now wash the Cat's Eye ring, apply sandal and kumkum and place it over the cloth.

Recite Ketu Mantra 108 times. After that, offer curd as offering. Wear the ring and donate sugar to somebody along with the bowl.

Ketu Mantra

> *Ashwa Dwajaaya Vidhmahe*
> *Shoola Hasthaaya Dheemahi*
> *Tanno Ketu Prachodayath*

Pooja for Substitute Gems

1. Pooja for Golden Topaz, Garnet, Surya Kantmani, Amber, Peridot etc.

Day & Time: Sunday, between 6am and 7am.

Method

Take a red silk cloth. Spread wheat over it. Wash the ring, apply chandan, kumkum to it and place it on the wheat. Offer agarbatti, camphor and red flowers. Recite the mantra given below 108 times and wear it.

Surya Mantra

Om Gruni Suryaya Namaha

2. Jade, Moon Stone

Day & Time: Monday or Poornima, 6-7am.

Method

Take a white silk cloth. Spread rice and sugar over it. Wash the ring and apply sandal, kumkum to it. Place it on the rice and sugar mixture. Offer agarbatti, camphor and white flowers. Recite the mantra given below 108 times and wear.

Moon Mantra

Om Som Somaya Namaha

3. Yellow Topaz, Amethyst, Yellow Zircon, Yellow Agate, Yellow Tourmaline

Day & Time: Thursday, between 6am and 7am.

Method

Take yellow silk cloth. Spread Bengal gram on it. Wash the ring and apply sandal and kumkum to it. Place it on the Bengal gram. Offer agarbatti, camphor along with yellow flowers and recite the mantra given below 108 times and wear it.

Guru Mantra

Om Brum Bruhaspataye Namaha

4. Jaichint, Hessonite Garnet

Day & Time: Wednesday, 6-7am.

Method

Take a brown silk cloth. Place back urad dal on it. Wash the ring and apply sandal and kumkum to it. Place it on the black urad dal and offer agarbatti, camphor and rose flowers and recite the mantra given below 108 times and wear it.

Rahu Mantra

Om Hraam Rahuve Namaha

5. Aquamarine, Green Onyx, Malachite, Green Zircon, Green Tourmaline

Day & Time: Wednesday, 6-7am.

Method

Take a green cloth. Spread green moong dal over it. Wash the ring and apply sandal, kumkum and place it over the green moong dal. Offer white flowers, agarbatti and camphor. Recite the Budha Mantra given below 108 times and wear the ring.

Budha Mantra

Om Bhum Budhaaya Namaha

6. White Zircon, White Tourmaline, Spathic, White Opal Turquoise etc.

Day & Time: Friday, 6-7am.

Method

Take a white silk cloth. Spread Rajmah over it. Apply sandal, kumkum to the ring and place it on the white silk. Offer white flowers, agarbatti and camphor. Recite the Mantra given below 108 times and wear the ring.

Shukra Mantra

Om Shum Shukraya Namaha

Tiger Eye

Day & Time: Wednesday, 6-7am.

Method

Take a red silk cloth. Spread horse gram over it. Apply sandal and kumkum etc. to the ring and place it on the red silk. Offer red flowers, agarbatti and camphor. Recite the Ketu Mantra given below 108 times and wear the ring.

Ketu Mantra

Om Kem Ketave Namaha

8. **Blue Zircon, Blue Tourmaline, Neelam, Lolit, Blue Star Ruby, Lapis Lazuli etc.**

Day & Time: Saturday, 6-7am.

Method

Spread a blue silk and place black til on it. Apply chandan and kumkum to the ring and place on the black til. Offer blue flowers, camphor, agarbatti. Recite the following mantra 108 times and wear the ring.

Saturn Mantra

Om Sham Shanaischaraya Namaha

9. **Red Cornelian, Red Tourmaline, Fire Opal, Red Jasper etc.**

Day & Time: Tuesday, 6-7am.

Method

Spread red silk cloth. Place tuar dal on it. Apply chandan and kumkum to the ring after washing the ring. Apply camphor, red flowers and agarbatti. Recite the following Mantra 108 times and wear the ring.

Mars Mantra

Om Aam Angaarakaya Namaha

10
Gems and Diseases

How Do Gems Cure the Diseases?

Our body is composed of seven colours of the solar spectrum. They are Violet, Indigo, Blue, Green, Yellow, Orange and Red. These are the basic colours, and other shades are made by mixing one or two of these colours. When there is a deficiency or absence of any one of these primary colours in our body, we get attacked by the disease caused by that deficiency. If the red rays are absent, diseases like anemia, fever, inflammation, general debility and weakness would afflict the body. These diseases can be cured by injecting red rays into our body, by wearing gems of red planets. The red planets are the Sun and Mars. Their gems are Ruby and Red Corals. When these gems come into contact with our body, they inject red rays into our body, whereby deficiency is restored, and we then become free from such diseases.

Again when there is an excess of red rays in our body, they produce diseases like boils, tumours, sunstroke, insomnia and headache etc. For curing these diseases the excess of red rays should be controlled to the normal limit. Even for controlling the red rays, the same Ruby and Red Coral should be worn. They neutralise the amount of red rays in our body, and we become free from such diseases.

How Does it Happen ?

The cosmic rays of each planet have a negative impact. They tend to effect us adversely. According to the date of birth, the human body can grasp only certain specific planetary vibrations. They relate to the birth number planet, fadic number planet, name number planet, and other planet, if negatively placed in the horoscope. These planets' negative currents fall on the human beings and produce adverse effects. By wearing these planets-specific gems, the malefic rays of such planets get filtered and only benefic rays are allowed to enter the body. The rays could be in excess or insufficient but the gems can neutralise the same and allow our body to get only a balanced quantity of rays, thereby causing those planets to produce only good effect. In this way, gems are working as guards for us.

Healing Power of the Gems

Certain gems have wonderful healing powers. Each gem cures certain diseases perfectly. They are:

1. **For prolonged vatha roga:** One should wear Blue Sapphire until the disease is completely cured.

2. **For nervous disorder and inflammation due to vatha:** One should wear Emerald until it is completely cured.

3. **For hip and joint pain, foot and arm pain:** One should wear Yellow Sapphire.

4. **For Liver Disorder, Jaundice:** Yellow Sapphire.
5. **For Drowsiness, Vomiting, Fever:** One should wear Cat's Eye.
6. **For Asthma, Bronchitis, T.B., Cold, Cough, Breathing trouble:** Wear White Pearl.
7. **For Anemia, Weakness:** Red Coral.
8. **For Heart Diseases:** Ruby or Emerald or Diamond.
9. **For Kidney Disorder:** Jade, Emerald or Rock Crystal.
10. **For Stomach Disorder:** Emerald.
11. **For Skin Diseases, Leprosy:** Gomeda.
12. **For Migraine Headache:** Star Sapphire or Jade.
13. **For Dental Problems:** Red Coral, Lapis Lazuli.
14. **For Ear, Nose, Throat Problems:** Yellow Sapphire, White Coral.
15. **For Urinary Problems:** Pearl, Diamond, Emerald, Red Coral, Yellow Sapphire, Topaz.
16. **For Blood Problems:** Blue Sapphire, Emerald, Ruby.
17. **For Sound Sleep:** Pearl, Moonstone, Yellow Topaz.
18. **For Blood Circulation, Heart & Digestion:** Ruby, Garnet, Star Ruby.
19. **For Tissue Problems, Tension:** Moonstone, Pearl.
20. **For Lungs & Nervous System:** Emerald, Peridot, Malachite, Jade.

21. **For curing Infectious Wounds:** Blue Sapphire, Amethyst.
22. **For controlling abortion:** Red Coral, Malachite.
23. **For constipation:** Red Coral.

11
Gems for Professional Success

Each profession is related to a planet and a gem. If that career-specific gem is worn, success in that profession is guaranteed.

Pearl: Those, who are in the business related to metals, engineering materials, computer, music or instrumental field, they should wear Pearl as their lucky gem.

Emerald: Those, who are in an agency, contract works, cloth business, oil business, decorative item, paper products, they should wear Emerald as their lucky gem.

Diamond: Those, who are in the administrative field, agriculture, dairy products, poultry farm, fruits and vegetable farm, should wear Diamond as their lucky gem.

Ruby: Those, who are in business related to Government, politics, social services, public welfare field, plays, acting and cinema, should wear Ruby as their lucky gem.

Red Coral: Those, who are in military, police, security service, real estate, hotel business, electrical business, should wear Red Coral as their lucky gem, for getting profits in the business.

Yellow Sapphire: Those, who are in the artistic, educational, financial, endowment fields or in religious or philosophical areas, should wear Yellow Sapphire as their lucky gem.

Blue Sapphire: Those, who are in the business of iron and steel, building materials, real estate, or are commission agents for purchasing and selling properties, should wear Blue Sapphire as their lucky gem.

Gomeda: Dancers, politicians, astrologers, tantriks, palmists should wear Gomeda as the gem for getting more profits in their business.

Cat's Eye: Lawyers, producers and directors, film actors and those in journalism, printers, medical field should wear Cat's Eye to get profits in their profession.

12

Auspicious Times and Metals for Wearing Gems

Auspicious Time for Wearing Precious Gems

1. **Moon Stones or White Pearl:** During the transit when the Moon is in Taurus. It should be set up in a silver ring and worn on a Monday.

2. **Red Coral:** During the transit when Mars is in Capricorn or Aries. It should be set in a gold or copper ring and worn on a Tuesday.

3. **Emerald:** During the transit when Mercury is in Virgo. It should be set in a gold ring and worn on a Wednesday.

4. **Diamond:** During the transit when Venus is in Taurus or in Pisces. It should be set in a platinum ring or a silver ring. It should be worn on a Friday.

5. **Yellow Sapphire:** During the transit when Jupiter is in Cancer. It should be set in a gold ring. It should be worn on a Thursday.

6. **Cat's Eye:** During the transit when Ketu is in Sagittarius. It should be set in a steel or a

silver ring and worn on a Wednesday, or a Saturday.

7. **Blue Sapphire:** During the transit when Saturn is in Libra. It should be set in a steel or a silver ring. It should be worn on a Saturday.

8. **Gomeda:** During the transit when Rahu is in Gemini. It should be set in a gold ring. It should be worn on a Wednesday.

9. **Ruby:** During the transit when the Sun is in Aries or Leo. It should be set in a gold ring and worn on a Sunday.

13
Crystals and Gems for the New Millennium

This section contains an alphabetical listing of one hundred or more crystals and gems. The arrangement is easy to follow. First, the stone is listed by its proper or common name. The crystal system in which the stone is found, comes next, followed by the cell salt, colour, energy, astrological attribution and their uses.

An attempt has been made to include as much information regarding each stone as possible; however, some of the entries contain more information than the others and some are not discussed earlier in the book. It is suggested that you use the following interpretations as a reference guide only and try to become personally familiar with the spirit of the stone in your possession.

AMBER

Crystal system: Amber is amorphous and not linked with any specific system.

Cell salt: It is not any specific cell salt. Amber is a fossil resin found in alluvian soils, coniferous trees and on some seashores.

Colour: Translucent yellow, honey-coloured, or brownish yellow resembling mummified insect and/or plant inclusions.

Energy: Electric.

Element: Fire.

Planet/sign: Sun/Leo; Mercury.

Uses: Amber may be used to increase vitality, motivation and creativity. It is a powerful amulet when worn for protection, especially when carved in the shape of your totem animal.

Wear Amber to attract warm, loyal and generous people into your life; or carry Amber on your person to lend logic or wit to a difficult situation.

Mixed with Turquoise, Amber is reminiscent of Sky Father or the Sun in the sky. This combination of energies may be used successfully to calm the mind and the nervous system.

Knock on wood three times with a natural piece of Amber to call on the spirits of the trees for special favours.

To increase prosperity, sew Amber and Turquoise along with several coins into a coyote skin pouch and bury the pouch in the earth.

Those having the Sun in Taurus or Scorpio should avoid Amber.

ANHYDRITE

Crystal system: Orthorhombic.

Cell salt: Calcium sulphate.

Colour: Ranges from white, grey, blue, red, or brick red to lavender; may appear translucent or fluorescent.

Energy: Electric.

Element: Fire.

Planet/sign: Mars-Pluto/Scorpio (exact cell salt equivalent); Sun/Leo.

Uses: The main function of Anhydrite is to assist in breaking down old habit patterns by bringing secrets buried deep within the soul to light. This stone will also open the heart centre by arousing sympathy for the human condition.

ANT HILL CRYSTALS

Crystal system: Hexagonal.

Cell salt: Silicon Dioxide.

Colour: Clear; sometimes translucent; milky white or beige.

Energy: Electric.

Element: Fire.

Planet/sign: Sagittarius/Jupiter.

Uses: Ant Hill Crystals expand and awaken the mind and soul through memory. These stones may be found at any ant hill; the bigger the ants, the larger the crystals.

Try this Ant Hill Crystal medicine: Gather Ant Hill Crystals; remembering to ask permission and thank the ants. Create your own rattle (an empty aluminium soft drink can work wonders). Place the Ant Hill Crystals inside and shake it about the house to clear a negative atmosphere. Or shake the rattle around your aura to clear out old emotional debris. The rattle may also be used for protection; the sound made by the Ant Hill Crystals keeps evil spirits at bay.

ANTIMONY

Crystal system: Orthorhombic.

Cell salt: Native, sometimes containing arsenic, iron and silver.

Colour: Tin-white to light steel-grey.

Energy: Electric.

Element: Fire.

Planet/sign: Sun/Leo.

Uses: This metallic mineral may be worn by the person for vitality, protection and improved blood circulation.

APATITE

Crystal system: Hexagonal.

Cell Salt: Calcium-fluorine-hydroxyl phosphate, often with small amounts of manganese and cerium.

Colour: Varying hues of green, brown, red, yellow, violet and pink, as well as white.

Energy: Electromagnetic.

Element: Fire, air and earth.

Planet/sign: Jupiter/Sagittarius; Mercury/Virgo.

Uses: Apatite is "mind over matter" stone. It helps to quieten emotional stress, especially during the more difficult phases of transformative incidents, such as divorce and death.

The influence of the green, brown, red, violet, pink, white and clear stones is dissolving, while that of pale yellow Apatite crystals, is resolving.

APHTITALITE

Crystal system: Hexagonal.

Cell salt: Potassium sulphate, often with other elements.

Colour: Colourless or white.

Energy: Neutral; magnetic.

Element: Air and fire.

Planet/sign: Mercury/Virgo (exact cell salt equivalent); also Jupiter/Sagittarius.

Uses: Aphtitalite may be used to promote unity and harmony of the body, mind and soul, as this stone balances the flow of cosmic energy throughout the body-earth. Use Aphtitalite when you are feeling down, to encourage feelings of contentment and self-assurance.

APOPHYLLITE

Crystal system: Tetragonal.

Cell salt: Hydrous calcium, potassium fluorosilicate, often with a small amount of iron and nickel.

Colour: Ranges from clear to white, grey, green, yellow and red, often with a pearly cast on cleavage.

Energy: Magnetic.

Element: Earth.

Planet/sign: Saturn/Capricorn; Mars/Aries; Mars-Pluto/Scorpio.

Uses: Use Apophyllite crystal to re-evaluate spiritual, mental, emotional and material resources and values. This stone brings victory through perseverance.

The clear and red crystals strengthen mental clarity and insight. Grey stones may be used to neutralize the opposition. Pale aqua or green Apophyllite may work to alter the cellular consciousness of body-earth by stimulating the reproductive organs through creative mental imagery.

ARSENIC

Crystal system: Hexagonal.

Cell salt: A native mineral ore, usually with some antimony, iron, nickel, silver and sulphur.

Colour: Tin white, quickly tarnishing to dark grey; evolved specimens are orange-red with a metallic glow.

Energy: Electric.

Element: Fire, air and earth.

Planet/sign: Jupiter/Sagittarius; Mercury/Virgo.

CAUTION: The fumes of arsenic crystal are poisonous, so take care to avoid breathing the fumes. Arsenic is deadly, if taken internally.

Uses: Despite the potential danger, this stone happens to be an excellent diagnostic tool for getting to the root of disruptive mental and physical conditions. It is especially beneficial when used to overcome inertia. The orange-red coloured crystals are the preferred healing stones.

AUTUNITE

Crystal system: Tetragonal.

Cell salt: Hydrous phosphate of calcium and uranium, often with some barium and magnesium.

Colour: Strongly fluorescent; lemon to sulphur yellow, yellow-green or green.

Energy: Magnetic.

Element: Earth.

Planet/sign: Saturn/Capricorn (closest cell salt equivalent).

Uses: Use Autunite crystal to stimulate creative imagination as well as to bring the mind under conscious control and direction.

This crystal works to open up the sight centre, thus enhancing the supersensory functions of hindsight, foresight and insight.

Lemon yellow Autunite crystals are the surest bet for raising sexual energy to the heart level. Yellow-green and green crystals reflect Earth energy and may be used to concentrate love within the heart centre.

Try this five-minute love medicine: Hold a yellow-green or green Autunite crystal in the open palm of your receptive hand. Relax and breathe deeply, inhaling and exhaling through the nose. Now, drop your awareness to your heart and continue breathing through the heart centre. Breathe in the love of Earth and all its creatures and things. Exhale love right back at them.

AZURITE (LAPIS LINGUIS)

Crystal system: Monoclinic.

Cell salt: Basic copper carbonate/copper ore.

Colour: Azure blue to dark blue; glossy and low-lustered.

Energy: Magnetic.

Element: Water.

Planet/sign: Moon; Venus.

Uses: Azurite crystals calm the emotional/auric energy field surrounding the body-earth. Wear Azurite on the person to produce sensations of empathy, compassion and love. It also aids meditation.

Deep azure blue specimens are favoured for developing psychic abilities through the pituitary centre or the third eye. Combined with Malachite crystal, Azurite may be used to soothe extreme anxiety affecting the back portion of the brain. It is thus an excellent alternative treatment for conditions such as anxiety attacks, panic disorder, anorexia and bulimia.

BARITE

Crystal system: Orthorhombic.

Cell salt: Barium sulphate, with small amounts of strontium.

Colour: White, grey, or colourless; or, yellow, brownish red, or blue, with vitreous and pearly lustre.

Energy: Electromagnetic.

Element: Earth and fire.

Planet/sign: Venus/Taurus; Sun/Leo; Mars-Pluto/Scorpio.

Uses: Barite crystal is a strong muscle stimulant. It may be used to alleviate the chills caused by hypothermia, fever and inflammation due to the agreeable sense of warmth it produces when placed in contact with the body.

Use Barite to raise your spirits during depression; laughter may occur if the stone is held in the hand long enough.

Try using Barite crystal during shamanic journey work or astral travel; this stone causes some sensitive individuals to feel as through they could fly through the air.

BERYL

Crystal system: Hexagonal.

Cell salt: Beryllium aluminum silicate, frequently with sodium, lithium and cerium.

Colour: Brilliant green (Emerald); blue, green-blue (Aquamarine); bright yellow (Golden Beryl); yellow-brown (Heliodor); red, pink (Morganite); white and colourless (Goshenite).

Uses: In general, Beryl increases psychic awareness and heightens human potential by expanding the mind to grasp the laws of Nature. It quickens the mind, cures inertia and rekindles romantic love in marital relationships. Its lordship is assigned to Venus and Mars.

This stone may also be used to enhance prophetic vision and to converse with water spirits.

There are many varieties of Beryl crystal, usually categorised according to colour. In all cases, Beryl should be set in a silver necklace, or set in silver and worn on the left ring finger.

> **AQUAMARINE** *crystal fosters acceptance of the transient nature of physical existence. The deep oceanic shades of aqua are best for transmutative purposes and may ease us through the process of death. This stone offers protection and courage. Pale blue or blue-green stones provide the wearer soothing calm.*

Aquamarine is the ultimate water divination stone. Place it in a crystal bowl filled with pure, natural spring water. Gaze deeply into the bowl and allow the images engendered through the stone to flow freely into consciousness.

Drink Aquamarine water as a tonic to enhance psychic awareness and mental clarity.

EMERALD *is perhaps the most popular and highly prized Beryl crystal. Brilliant green Emerald is an Earth Mother stone, a stone of Nature and therefore heightens our ability to be ecology-conscious.*

Creative imagination, prosperity, protection, love and fertility are increased by Emerald crystal. Wear an Emerald ring on the index finger of your receptive hand to relieve or prevent disease, or against the throat to gently calm and balance all seven-spirit energy centres at once.

Gaze at the Emerald to soothe tired eyes, or keep Emerald crystal in the northernmost corner of the home to keep out evil spirits.

The best Emerald crystals are found in India. Choose specimens that are coloured medium to dark transparent green or blue-green. Inclusions are common and do not negatively affect the quality of the stone.

GOLDEN BERYL *stimulates the heart, clears the mind and promotes genuine feelings of love and affection when worn in a ring on the third finger of the Sun or the fourth finger of Mercury on the receptive hand.*

GOSHENITE *is a memory stone. White Goshenite may be used to clear long-held emotional patterns lingering in the psyche; colourless Goshenite crystal assists in bringing the spirit of the cosmos to earth-plane consciousness.*

Use Goshenite to remember past lives and bless the ancestors. Hold Goshenite in the open palm of your

> *receptive hand. Breathe deeply and focus your attention behind you. Begin to pray for your relatives—first the living, then the dead. Follow the ancestral stream, allowing the images of family members to appear in your mind's eye. Bless and forgive each image that arises to the surface. Now hold the stone against your solar plexus as you bless and forgive yourself.*
>
> **HELIODOR** *crystal may be used as an aid to concentration in work to achieve a specific goal. Put raw, yellow-brown heliodor at the base of your favourite trees and shrubs and watch the plants grow tall and strong.*
>
> **MORGANITE** *may help resolve painful sexual issues regarding abuse and gender orientation. The purple-red stones accelerate self-forgiveness and self-love.*

BOJI STONE

Crystal system: Isometric.

Cell salt: Trace metals and elements including pyrite, palladium, fossil and petrified bone.

Colour: Black, varying to lighter shades of metallic silver grey iridescence.

Energy: Electric and magnetic.

Element: Air and water.

Planet/sign: Mercury/Gemini; Moon/Cancer; Saturn-Uranus/Aquarius.

Users: Boji stone gathers energy within its powerful electromagnetic field. The smooth, round stones are "female" and the rough, crystallized, odd-shaped stones are "male." It is good to acquire a healing pair.

Boji stone balances energy and removes blockages from the aura as well as the body. It also cleans, charges and fills up the holes in the aura.

Generally, this strange, heavy metallic ball is excellent for grounding subtle energies while establishing a harmonious polarity throughout the physical, emotional, mental and finer spirit bodies.

Boji stone works well when carried in a pouch. Hold the stones on the fingers of your receptive hand along with rock crystal to neutralize bad vibes.

BONE

Crystal system: None.

Cell salt: Calcium phosphate, calcium carbonate, calcium fluoride, calcium chloride and magnesium phosphate, with small amounts of sodium chloride and sulphate.

Colour: Dull white, greyish white, brownish white and darker shades of brown.

Energy: Magnetic.

Element: Earth.

Planet/sign: Saturn/Capricorn.

Uses: There are as many kinds of bones as there are fish reptiles, birds and animals. However, some types of bones are more popular or common than others.

CALCITE

Crystal system: Hexagonal.

Cell salt: Calcium carbonate.

Colour: White or colourless; pale shades of grey, yellow, red, blue and green; black to brown when impure.

Energy: Electromagnetic.

Element: Air and fire.

Planet/sign: Mercury/Virgo; Jupiter/Sagittarius.

Uses: Evolved specimens of Calcite crystal are clear and reflective, like a magic mirror. Clear Calcite crystal refracts light and doubles the energy of whatever it contacts with. Grey Calcite is a neutralising agent.

Yellow Calcite clears the mind. The red stones energize and tone the blood. Pink Calcite opens the heart to receive affection and love. Blue crystals may be used during purification and healing rituals. Green Calcite may be used as a money magnet or prosperity stone.

CHALCEDONY

Crystal system: Hexagonal.

Cell Salt: Silicon dioxide.

Colour: White to grey, brown, blue, black; clear red to brownish red (cornelian); bright green with red spots (Bloodstone/Heliotrope); variegated and banded (Agate); with mosslike or treelike inclusions (Moss Agate); apple-green (Chrysoprase); variegated and mottled red, yellow, brown (Jasper); whitish, dull grey, smoky brown to black (Flint) green-onyx.

Energy: Electric.

Element: Air and fire.

Planet/Sign: Mercury/Virgo; Jupiter/Sagittarius.

Uses: In general, Chalcedony gives success in lawsuits, good health, safe travels and protects against harmful spirits. However, there are many varieties of Chalcedony crystals, each with its own particular properties.

CHRYSOBERYL

Crystal system: Orthorhombic.

Cell salt: Beryllium aluminium oxide, often with small amounts of iron and chromium.

Colour: Yellow-green to deep green; blue-green (Alexandrite); green-white, green-brown and yellow (Cat's Eye).

Energy: Magnetic and electric.

Element: Earth and fire.

Planet/sign: Venus/Taurus; Sun/Leo; Mars-Pluto/Scorpio.

Uses: Chysoberyl raises sexual energy from the lower bodily centres up to the heart level. It enables the wearer to respond to others with genuine feelings of kindness and affection.

ALEXANDRITE, *a brownish green variety, encourages receptivity and surrender to the forces of Nature. Blue-green Alexandrite teaches self-discipline and control; it may also bring luck in love as it harmonizes opposing male and female energies within the relationship.*

CAT'S EYE *is an ancient Asian stone with many uses. The uppermost branches of the Hindu world tree were said to be made of Cat's Eye hinting that this stone may be used to see into the future or communicate with the spiritual world.*

Cat's Eye has long been touted as a health and beauty aid. Place a Cat's Eye in spring water overnight and drink the liquid in the morning as a tonic. This stone epitomizes the phrase "live long and prosper." Wear Cat's Eye to increase longevity as well as for prosperity.

CHRYSOCHOLLA (LAPIS LINGUA)

Crystal system: Monoclinic.

Cell salt: Basic copper silicate.

Colour: Green, blue-green; brown to black (from impurities in the stone).

Energy: Magnetic.

Element: Earth and water.

Planet/sign: Venus-Neptune/Pisces.

Uses: Chrysocholla works directly on the cells of the body to heal inflammation and disease.

Use Chrysocholla to bless the past and forgive past hurts and disappointments. This will release the cells that hold onto sickness and clear the way for healthy new cells to regenerate the tissue and organs within the body-earth. Gemmologists use them in occult and mystical healing.

CORUNDUM

Crystal system: Hexagonal.

Cell salt: Aluminium oxide.

Colour: White, grey; brown to black; deep red (Ruby); blue (Sapphire); black, from a mixture of magnetite, hematite or spinel (Emery).

Energy: Electric.

Element: Air and fire.

Planet/sign: Mercury/Virgo; Jupiter/Sagittarius.

Uses: Corundum provides a cure for all the ills of the world. There are several colourful varieties of Corundum, each with its own healing properties.

EMERY *is Saturn stone; use it for grounding and focusing your attention on a particular subject. This black stone is also an excellent aid for self-evaluation; it will help you get to the root of the problem fast.*

RUBY *gives a general sense of well-being throughout the body-earth. It can remove evil thoughts and worries, control the sexual appetite and resolve disputes.*

The Chinese people believe Ruby confers long life. The use of Ruby gives great joy and good fortune.

Ruby was once thought to make the wearer invulnerable to wounds, especially if the skin was pierced with the stone. Wear Ruby on the left side of the body, or on the index or little finger of the receptive hand, as a shield against misfortune; or incorporate Ruby in jewellery as a body-piercing adornment for added protection and power.

Ruby develops a sympathetic rapport with the owner of the stone and tends to fade in colour if neglected for too long. Dark red rubies are "male," while the lighter stones are "female." Should you be drawn to Ruby, try to acquire a mated pair.

For maximum strength, wear Ruby on the left ring finger set in either gold or silver.

SAPPHIRE *lives in the roots of the Hindu world tree. It was once considered an ancestral stone, enabling the wearer to see into the world soul.*

The Sapphire represents wisdom, magnanimous thoughts, love, good manners and vigilance. Kings would wear the Sapphire around their necks to protect them from any harm.

Because Sapphire is a clear, pure blue colour like the sky, church fathers consider it to have a godly nature and it is, therefore, considered as a "sacred" gem.

Sapphire has the power to influence the spirits; it is a tonic to counteract negative witchcraft and attract good spirits. It was, therefore, a great favourite among sorcerers. *The Star Sapphire, which is milky or greyish blue, is the best guard against the evil eye. This stone may help cure certain diseases of the physical eyes as well.*

Ayurvedic healers recommend Sapphire for diseases such as rheumatism, sciatica, neurological pain, epilepsy, hysteria and all nerve disorders, especially when set in gold and worn around the neck.

Sapphire will sometimes change colour if the person wearing the stone has an unfaithful nature. Gaze at this stone for several minutes as a preparation for meditation to help quieten and compose a racing, disturbed mind.

DIAMOND

Crystal system: Isometric.

Cell salt: Carbon.

Colour: Colourless, clear; light yellow, brown, green, blue; deep brown, orange, violet, yellow, yellow-green, red, blue and deep green.

Energy: Electric.

Element: All.

Planets: Saturn and Mercury.

Uses: Attention, discrimination, recollection, receptivity, inspiration, faith, endurance and concentration are the mental/emotional responses elicited via our relationship with Diamond.

It is good for sleep-walkers. If constantly worn, it promotes constancy in marriage. It protects against witchcraft, evil forces and satanism.

Because the Diamond is capable of regenerating and reintegrating the body-earth, it may be worn as a reminder of our integral wholeness and spiritual perfection.

Diamond shields the wearer from negative projections and the machinations of others. Try a Diamond instead of a rock crystal ball to peer into the future.

The Diamond can be used as heart tonic. Place it in a glass of water overnight and drink the liquid the following day.

Pink or red Diamond promotes feelings of love and affection. The blue Diamond may bring tranquillity in stressful situations. Green Diamond has a soothing, calming effect on the central nervous system and the physical body in general. Breadth of vision and enthusiasm is inspired by violet Diamond. Orange increases vital energy, while yellow enables the wearer to transmit healing light.

Diamond should be set in gold and worn on the right middle finger. Avoid poor-quality Diamonds, as these may cast an adverse effect on your health.

DIOPSIDE

Crystal system: Monoclinic.

Cell salt: Calcium, magnesium silicate.

Colour: White, colourless, grey, or green.

Energy: Magnetic.

Element: Earth and water.

Planet/sign: Venus-Neptune/Pisces.

Uses: This mineral clears out congested emotions by circulating cosmic energy throughout the auric field.

Diopside increases creative visualisation and helps manifest desired goals. Clear or light green gem-quality crystals are preferred when using this stone for visionary purposes. Hold Diopside on the third eye or pituitary centre when conjuring mental images and notice the clarity with which they appear.

Also, wear Diopside on the person between the throat and heart centres to attract love into your life.

DIOPTASE

Crystal system: Hexagonal.

Cell salt: Basic copper silicate.

Colour: Deep vivid green.

Energy: Magnetic.

Element: Earth.

Planet/sign: Venus; Mercury/Virgo; Jupiter/Sagittarius.

Uses: Dioptase crystal opens up and expands the gateways of the mind. It prepares us to receive affection and love from all our relationships, the Earth and the cosmos. Wear this stone to bring abundance, prosperity, creativity, peace and good health into your life.

EPIDOTE

Crystal system: Monoclinic.

Cell salt: Basic calcium, aluminium and iron silicate.

Colour: Yellowish-green to brownish black.

Energy: Magnetic.

Element: Water.

Planet/sign: Neptune/Pisces; Virgo.

Uses: The Epidote is a mediating influence and may be carried on or about the person to ensure protection against conflicting circumstances. It soothes the emotionally and physically disturbed bodies, composes the mind and lessens the frequency of panic and/or pangs of anxiety.

Epidote also works to heal intestinal blockages due to nervous disorders affecting the stomach.

Epidote has recently entered a renewed stage of accelerated evolutionary growth and will soon be recognized as an important agent in the self-healing process.

Greenish black and pistachio-coloured stones are most favourable for reflecting, conducting and projecting healing Earth energy back into the environment.

FLUORITE

Crystal system: Isometric.

Cell salt: Calcium fluoride.

Colour: Violet, blue, green, yellow, brown, blue-black, pink, rose-red, colourless and white.

Energy: Electromagnetic.

Element: Air and water.

Planet/sign: Mercury/Gemini; Saturn-Uranus/Aquarius; Moon/Cancer (exact cell salt equivalent).

Uses: The element of air predominates in this mineral substance. Use it to increase mental agility when attempting to analyse important information.

This New Millennium stone emphasises the concerns of ancestral connections, the immediate home and family and our inter-connection with the Earth. While Fluorite impresses us at personal levels, it also conducts energy from the upper world of spirit to the lower world of soul. Generally, Fluorite is helpful for easing emotional problems, especially those arising on the home front.

Fluorite is associated with fluoride and may be used to strengthen the teeth and bones and prevent their decay.

Violet crystals promote mental expansion, allowing us to view ourselves and our actions from a higher vantage point. Blue Fluorite benefits any situation requiring clear communication. Green Fluorite may help to heal troubled relationships. Pink and rose-red stones are stimulating and revitalising and may be used to dispel feelings of inertia. Brown or black crystals aid concentration, while the white or colourless varieties provide a protective shield of influence throughout the auric and physical bodies. Pictures and images held inside the stone, such as clouds, trees, or angels also suggest the purpose of the stone in your possession.

GARNET

Crystal system: Isometric.

Cell salt: Aluminium silicates (Pyrope, Almandine and Spessartine) and calcium silicates (Grossular, Andradite and Uvarovite).

Colour: Deep red to reddish black (Pyrope); deep red to brown or brownish black (Almandine); brownish red to hyacinth red (Spessartine); colourless, white, yellow, pink, green or brown (Grossular); wine red or greenish (Andradite); emerald green (Uvarovite).

Energy: Electromagnetic.

Element: Air and water.

Planet/sign: Mercury/Gemini; Moon/Cancer; Saturn-Uranus/Aquarius.

Uses: In general, Garnet should be set in gold for individuals with nervous or sluggish dispositions, while active people should wear Garnet set in silver.

ALMANDINE *was associated with Bacchus, the Roman god of wine. Tonic water prepared with Almandine may be helpful in easing hangover symptoms. Place the stone in a bowl of purified water, let it stand overnight and drink upon waking.*

ANDRADITE *unearths buried secrets. Take this stone with you when mining, beachcombing, or looking for lost objects. Give an Andradite crystal to your lover and listen carefully to what he or she reveals to you.*

GROSSULAR *increases our receptivity to the images held in Nature—sky, clouds, Sun's rays, moonbeams and the green and growing things of Earth. This stone liberates the human spirit via its soothing, grounding and calming effects on the emotional body.*

PYROPE *contains living fire and works to release outworn habit patterns by destroying the erroneous ideas and emotions that keep us enslaved to guilt and fear. Pyrope clears the way for new beginnings.*

This stone has long been recognized for its use as an anti-inflammatory and blood-clotting agent.

SPESSARTINE *inspires enthusiasm, refines one's manners, heightens awareness, sharpens the tongue and lends personal grace and charm in dealings with the public.*

UVAROVITE *stands for growth, peace, prosperity and abundance. Wear it against the lower belly as a fertility charm or use it as a meditation aid to promote world peace.*

GYPSUM

Crystal system: Monoclinic.

Cell salt: Hydrous calcium sulphate.

Colour: White, colourless (selenite); grey, yellow, red or brown with a pearlized lustre on the cleavage of the stone.

Energy: Magnetic.

Element: Earth and water.

Planet/sign: Venus-Neptune/Pisces.

Uses: Gypsum brings protection and good fortune. It is an excellent tool for developing mental telepathy. It has the effects of the Cat's Eye.

SELENITE, the transparent variety of Gypsum, may be used to strengthen and preserve the memory.

HALITE

Crystal system: Isometric.

Cell salt: Sodium chloride (salt).

Colour: Colourless or tinted with grey, yellow, red or blue.

Energy: Electromagnetic.

Element: Fire.

Planet/sign: Jupiter/Sagittarius (exact cell salt equivalent); Mercury/Gemini; Moon/Cancer; Saturn-Uranus/Aquarius.

Uses: Halite crystal is actually solidified salt. Use it for grounding, protection, or to block negative energies.

If someone is causing you harm, write his or her name nine times on a piece of white paper. Fold the paper into small square and cover it completely with the Halite cube. This won't hurt the other person, but it will stop them in their tracks and won't be able to harm you. For added protection, place a Halite crystal in each of the four corners of your house—north, south, east and west.

HOWLITE

Crystal system: Monoclinic.

Cell salt: Hydrated calcium silico-borate.

Colour: Dull, glimmering white.

Energy: Magnetic.

Element: Earth and water.

Planet/sign: Venus-Neptune/Pisces.

Uses: Howlite reflects and transfers spirit energy throughout the body-earth and cleanses the mind and emotions of negative thoughts and images.

This stone functions best when placed on a table or shelf, in close proximity to a well-frequented area.

JADE (JADEITE OR NEPHRITE)

Crystal system: Monoclinic.

Cell salt: Sodium aluminum silicate, often with some calcium and iron.

Colour: Yellow, apple green, emerald green (Imperial Jade) to white and translucent (Jadeite).

Energy: Magnetic.

Element: Earth and water.

Planet/sign: Venus-Neptune/Pisces.

Uses: American Indians use Jade to heal all ailments associated with the kidneys as well as to aid in childbirth. Jade may be worn when treating gallstones, the lungs, the heart and the throat as well.

Set in gold and silver jewellery, Jade is thought to prolong life and bring abundant riches to the wearer.

A Chinese tonic, made of powdered Jade, rice and rainwater when boiled in a copper pot and carefully filtered through a fine mesh to remove all impurities, may strengthen the muscles, harden the bones, quieten the mind, tone the skin and clean the blood.

CAUTION: Do not attempt this treatment without the guidance of qualified ayurvedic professional.

IMPERIAL JADE contains extremely powerful remedial abilities for relieving renal disorders due to its apple or emerald green colouring.

JAROSITE

Crystal system: Hexagonal.

Cell salt: Basic hydrous potassium iron sulphate.

Colour: Cloudy amber, yellow, or dark brown.

Energy: Electric.

Element: Earth and air.

Planet/sign: Mercury/Virgo (exact cell salt equivalent); Jupiter/Sagittarius.

Uses: Jarosite brings dark or incomprehensible thoughts and ideas into sharp focus. Use this stone when contemplating both the shadow and light sides of your personality.

LAZURITE (LAPIS LAZULI)

Crystal system: Isometric (Lazurite is a part of the Sodalite group of minerals, though softer, lighter and more finely grained).

Cell salt: Silicate of sodium calcium and aluminium, with some sulphur (when Lazurite also contains large amounts of calcite, diopside and pyrite, it is called Lapis Lazuli.)

Colour: Azure-blue, violet-blue and greenish blue.

Energy: Magnetic.

Element: Water.

Planet/sign: Moon/Cancer; Mercury/Gemini; Saturn-Uranus/Aquarius.

Uses: Lapis Lazuli may be used to cure depression, sadness, mourning and grief, as this stone exerts a strong influence in matters of the heart, including faithfulness and love. It may be used to treat physical heart conditions as well.

Lapis can keep the eyes healthy and the vision clear. Prepare an eyewash by placing Lapis in a bowl of purified water overnight along with several drops of the herb. In the morning, splash the treated water into your eyes.

Lapis increases the psychic senses, as it works to fine-tune the feelings and instincts. Deep azure-blue, pyrite-streaked stones are potent healing medicines when worn with purposeful intent and may help the wearer develop clairsentient and telepathic powers.

Vedic healers suggest that Lapis be set into a gold necklace for optimum benefits.

MALACHITE

Crystal system: Monoclinic.

Cell salt: Basic copper carbonate.

Colour: Emerald green, grass green and dark green.

Energy: Magnetic.

Element: Earth and water.

Planet/sign: Venus-Neptune/Pisces.

Uses: Malachite may induce feelings of sympathy and compassion for others. If worn consistently, it will restore vitality and life to a melancholy disposition.

We benefit from the soothing sensations of maternal warmth and love emanating from Malachite crystal. However, Malachite has a tendency to absorb negativity when used for healing purposes. Therefore, it must be thoroughly cleared and recharged after each use, or else, it will fade and eventually begin to crack from retaining poisons and disease. The earth clearing method, outlined in chapter 7, is best suited for Malachite as this stone regains strength and re-establishes equilibrium in the moist, fertile loam of Mother Earth.

MARCASITE

Crystal system: Orthorhombic.

Cell salt: Disulfide of iron.

Colour: Pale brass-yellow to almost white metallic glitter.

Energy: Magnetic.

Element: Earth and fire.

Planet/sign: Venus-Neptune/Taurus; Sun/Leo; Mars-Pluto/Scorpio.

Uses: Although Marcasite crystals are in the process of dissolution, the existing polished specimens retain strong Earth energy and the power to calm the mind and instill emotional stability. Wear Marcasite set in silver jewellery for optimum benefits.

META-ANKOLEITE

Crystal system: Tetragonal.

Cell salt: Potassium phosphate.

Colour: Yellow.

Energy: Electric.

Element: Fire.

Planet/sign: Mars-Pluto/Aries (exact cell salt equivalent); Saturn/Capricorn.

Uses: Meta-ankoleite is difficult to obtain. However, should you get your hands on it, its healing energy resonates predominantly within the body-earth, as it purifies the blood and strengthens the central nervous system through the cellular groups in the head, heart and sacral areas.

MOLDAVITE

Crystal system: Hexagonal.

Cell salt: Moldavite falls into a subgroup of stones called tektites, which are silica based, or glassy meteorites.

Colour: Translucent olive green.

Energy: Electric.

Element: Air and fire.

Planet/sign: Mercury/Virgo; Jupiter/Sagittarius.

Uses: Moldavite allows us to reach the deeper levels of conscious awareness. I have found it to be a more effective medicine for those who have practised some serious form of self-discipline, such as martial arts or spiritual pathwork.

The Otherworld quality of Moldavite mesmerizes and quietens the senses. Use it to increase your knowledge of the relationship between heaven and Earth.

This stone works well with Crystal, Sugilite, Aquamarine, Diamond, Lapis Lazuli, Opal and Peridot.

MOONSTONE

Crystal system: Monoclinic.

Cell salt: Potassium aluminium silicate, sometimes with large amounts of sodium.

Colour: Transparent; opalescent; moon-like, silvery white light.

Energy: Magnetic.

Element: Water.

Planet/sign: Moon; Venus-Neptune/Pisces.

Uses: Due to the moving spirit-light inside the stone, moonstone is a trance-inducing gem and may be used for hypnotherapy, scrying and all manner of divinatory work.

As in earlier times, the moonstone may be used to instill tender passion in the hearts of lovers. Place moonstone in your mouth during a full moon to read what the future holds for your love relationship.

Certain moonstones can be used to mark the waxing and waning of the moon. Observe your moonstone for about a month by following the moving light within the stone. The light should appear as a small point on top of the stone during the new moon, as a round dot in the centre during the full moon and as a small point at the bottom of the stone during the last quarter moon.

Moonstone set in a silver ring should be worn on the right ring finger of a person who frequently suffers from emotional upsets during the new or full moon.

NEWBERYITE

Crystal system: Orthorhombic.

Cell salt: Magnesium phosphate.

Colour: Grey, brown, or colourless.

Energy: Electric.

Element: Fire.

Planet/sign: Sun/Leo (exact cell salt equivalent); Venus-Neptune/Taurus; Mars-Pluto/Scorpio.

Uses: Newberyite dissolves old habit patterns and encourages the development of new and constructive thoughts, images and actions.

Use this stone to strengthen the heart muscle, improve blood circulation and to relieve pressure on the spine resulting from a back injury.

OBSIDIAN

Crystal system: Obsidian is an amorphous solid of glass substance formed from volcanic lava.

Cell salt: Spherulites of feldspar fibres with crystalline silica.

Colour: Generally black with smoky, translucent to transparent edges; also black mixed with grey, reddish brown, mahogany, dark green, forming thin bands or marbled.

Energy: Magnetic.

Element: Earth and fire.

Planet/Sign: Saturn; Mars-Pluto.

Uses: Round spheres of Obsidian are still sold in Mexico today. Use them in place of clear quartz crystal for divinatory purposes.

Obsidian can aid the decision-making process. It is capable of both attracting and repelling negativity and must, therefore, be used with care. This stone is excellent for grounding and all situations wherein you are forced to undergo drastic changes beyond your control.

APACHE TEARS are a natural, rough, circular, or cylindrical form of Obsidian. These dense black crystals may be carried in a medicine pouch or set in silver jewellery as a powerful protective amulet against all negative influences.

OPAL

Crystal system: Opal is an amorphous stone and not linked with any specific system.

Cell salt: Hydrous silica, often with some iron and aluminium.

Colour: White (White Opal); Yellow, red, pink (Fire Opal); brown, green grey, or blue flames in a black field (Black Opal); pale blue, green, orange (Precious Opal); colourless.

Energy: Neutral-electric.

Element: Air.

Planet/sign: All.

Uses: The Opal has been gravely misunderstood. It is difficult to wear because it is very fragile and needs special care and conscious attention. If you wear an Opal ring, for example, be careful not to bang your hand against a hard surface, or the stone may break.

The key to understanding Opal is balance. Like the Malachite, Opal will crack if you are out of sync, in danger, or under stress. For this reason, wear Opal to ensure your safety and to protect your position against those who wish you harm, or simply to bring good fortune.

Opal may be used to cure eye diseases as well as to render the wearer invisible.

The natural, youthful lustre of hair may be maintained by wearing Opal barrettes or earrings that touch the hair in some way. If the stone begins to fade, you may need to increase your vitamin intake or change your shampoo to keep your hair looking shiny and healthy.

Wear Opal on the right index finger in a gold ring, or set in a gold necklace.

BLACK OPAL is an exceptionally lucky stone. However, it may also bring us to the brink of the abyss where dwells the shadow self who must be faced if we are to realise who we are and why we are here.

FIRE OPAL contains the energies of all the heavenly bodies. Use it to balance the seven-spirit energy centres, or to assist you in astral projection or shamanic journey work.

PRECIOUS OPAL flares with the gentle spirit of love. This form of Opal may be used in all healing work. It is an especially valuable stone for the healer as a diagnostic tool, for the colours of the stone will fade out when it is swept over a troublesome auric or body area.

WHITE OPAL is a powerful supersensory receiver of lunar energies. It is also an excellent medicinal stone for the treatment of skin inflammations such as boils, pimples and rashes and for general elimination of toxins from the body. Opal does not suit those whose Venus is malefic in their horoscope.

PERIDOT

Crystal system: Orthorhombic.

Cell salt: Magnesium iron silicate.

Colour: Yellow-green; dark yellow-green (Olivine).

Energy: Electric.

Element: Earth and fire.

Planet/sign: Venus/Taurus; Sun/Leo; Mars-Pluto/Scorpio.

Uses: Peridot is both a receiver and transmitter of healing energy. It is a helpful agent in clearing emotional and physical congestion.

There is a connection between Peridot and the digestive, assimilative and eliminatory systems and it may be used to bring light into the dark, hidden regions of the bowel.

While Peridot is strong and resistant, it has been known to sustain damage if the central nervous system is unduly stressed or permeated with atmospheric, auric, or physical toxins. Many years ago, the Peridot set into my quartz crystal pendulum became chipped at a time when I was under extreme duress. The stone had absorbed all the bad vibes that were transmitted in my direction. I worked to clear the energy from the stone and could not use it for a long time thereafter. One day, several years later, I once again picked up the pendulum. Upon close inspection, the chip was no longer visible. The stone had healed and once again enjoys gainful employment as a divinatory tool and protective amulet.

OLIVINE is a darker close relative of Peridot crystal. The same medicinal uses apply to Olivine.

PIPESTONE (CATLINITE)

Crystal system: Isometric.

Cell salt: Hydrous aluminium silicate.

Colour: Brick red.

Energy: Magnetic.

Element: Earth, air and fire.

Planet/sign: Mercury/Gemini; Moon/Cancer; Saturn-Uranus/Aquarius.

Uses: Pipestone is used primarily to fashion the sacred pipe, which is always handled with utmost respect. The bowl is filled with *canshasha*, the red willow bark tobacco, or herbs such as sage or wild cherry bark. Then the pipe is lit and the smoke offered to grandfather sky, grandmother earth and to the four directions. As the pipe is shared among the people, the smokers become one with the earth and sky, because they are filled with the great mystery of visible breath.

If you wear Pipestone beads or keep a piece of natural Pipestone in the medicine pouch, recognise that it is a great blessing to have this stone in your possession! Always treat Pipestone with utmost respect and remember to include the Lakota and all indigenous people in your thanksgiving.

POTTERY SHERDS

Crystal system: Isometric.

Cell salt: Hydrous aluminium silicate.

Colour: Creamy white; reddish brown; black; often with hand-painted surfaces.

Energy: Magnetic.

Element: Earth.

Planet/sign: Mercury/Gemini; Moon/Cancer; Saturn-Uranus/Aquarius.

PYRITE

Crystal system: Isometric.

Cell salt: Iron disulphide, often with substantial amounts of nickel and cobalt.

Colour: Pale to brass-yellow, sometimes tarnished with a brownish film of iron oxide.

Energy: Electric.

Element: Air.

Planet/sign: Mercury/Gemini; Moon/Cancer; Saturn-Uranus/Aquarius.

Uses: Polished Pyrite is an excellent divinatory tool. It may also be used to focus the attention, transmit healing energy, or to attract money and good health.

QUARTZ

Crystal system: Hexagonal.

Cell salt: Silicon dioxide.

Colour: Colourless and transparent (Rock Crystal); clear with rutile inclusions (Rutilated); clear with black inclusions (Tourmalinated Quartz); purple (Amethyst); pink, rose-red (Rose Quartz); clear yellow (Citrine); pale brown to black (Smoky Quartz); milk-white (Milky Quartz); glistening green with mica or hematite inclusions (Aventurine); opalescent with asbestos inclusions (Cat's Eye); lustrous yellow to brown (Tiger's Eye).

Energy: Electric.

Element: Fire and air.

Planet/sign: Sagittarius (exact cell salt equivalent); Mercury/Virgo.

Uses: Many spiritual practitioners, from traditional shamans to contemporary healers, have the versatile Quartz crystal in their possession. Indeed, the remedial uses of this stone are many. It can be taken internally when formulated into an elixir (see chapter 5, Crystal Medicine 5: Sun and Moon Water tonic for Wholeness of Being), worn as jewellery, carried in a medicine pouch, or combined with metals and other stones to be fashioned into various transformational tools.

AMETHYST has an extensive history and is a marvellous healing crystal. The Egyptians made Amethyst amulets in the form of animals as early as 2000 B.C. The Hebrews believed that this stone could induce dreams and visions, while the Greeks thought it could prevent drunkenness.

Amethyst has the power to control all types of harmful behaviour, sharpen the mind, improve the memory and strengthen the immune system. It is able to calm an overly passionate nature. This stone may also protect soldiers from harm and help hunters find food in the wild.

All physical, emotional and mental problems may be treated with Amethyst. The deep purple variety is an excellent stone for hospice and hospital workers, as Amethyst helps to alleviate the emotional sense of attachment to the body-earth for those about to cross over to the Otherworld.

AVENTURINE is a Nature stone. It brings peace, tranquillity and serenity when used as touchstone and may be used to attract abundance and prosperity when worn on the body or carried in a medicine pouch.

CAT'S EYE QUARTZ is not quite as distinct as the Chrysoberyl Cat's Eye. However, the stone may be used to the same effect.

CITRINE was a prized stone among Celtic and Scottish peoples. It is energizing, invigorating and positive. It increases motivation and relieves feelings of inertia, thereby improving digestion and clearing congestion from the internal organs. Citrine may purify blood as well.

Citrine may be used as blessing stone to offer love and gratitude to the Great Spirit, as well as to open the heart centre. It magnifies thoughts and emotions and can assist in manifesting desires.

There is a special correspondence between Citrine and the element of air. It is therefore extremely beneficial in clearing negative atmospheres. Use Citrine as a touchstone to instill warmth and love following treatment of panic disorders, anxiety attacks, fears, phobias and obsessions.

Avoid purchasing stones that have been heat processed. Obtain only deep yellow crystals without any traces of purple colouring.

HERKIMER DIAMOND comes from Herkimer, New York. This stone is a very old storehouse of ecological memory. It acts as a filter to release toxins from the body-earth as well as boosting the immune system. Use it to increase the energy and healing qualities of other stones.

MILKY QUARTZ is not a very popular stone, probably due to its dense, white colour. However, it symbolizes the here and now and may help those following a spiritual path to recognize life as an eternal process. If you work with a Milky Quartz long enough, the stone will eventually become clear as Rock Crystal and so will you.

ROCK CRYSTAL, also known as crystal or as white crystal, is the most popular form of quartz. Shamans have used Rock Crystal for hundreds of years because it grants them the power to rise to the sky, or fly to the top of the World Tree!

This stone amplifies whatever influences are present in a particular person, place, or thing. It is a dedicated healer and may be used to remove physical, emotional, mental and spiritual blockages. It directs energy into sluggish auric and body areas to accelerate the healing process. Rock crystal can be worn or used by anyone for any purpose imaginable, or used in conjunction with other crystals, gems and minerals to treat specific problems. It will magnify the effects of individual stones and adjust the healing medicine to suit individual energy needs.

Sometimes, the high vibrational frequencies and the strong electromagnetic currents of energy emitted through Rock Crystal may increase emotional sensitivity and activate the central nervous system of highly receptive individuals. If you start to feel "burned out" from overexposure, remove it from contact with the body, wrap it in silk or deer hide and place it on your night table until your body adjusts to the increased energy levels engendered by the stone.

ROSE QUARTZ imparts a gentle, soothing influence and is especially beneficial for calming the emotions. It is quite restorative when healing old traumatic memories and wounds stemming from childhood abuse, abandonment, neglect, separation or divorce.

Rose Quartz makes an excellent gift for lovers, children and anyone in need of sympathy and affection. Choose pale, translucent shades of pink radiating with rainbow infractions for this purpose.

RUTILATED QUARTZ contains needle-like rutile inclusions (see RUTILE). The energy of rutile is magnified by the quartz for stepped up healing benefits. See Rutile for further information.

SMOKY QUARTZ is a stone of the lower world of soul. This stone was once popular among crystal gazers. It can be used when praying to heal ancestors and may be carried by people undergoing chemotherapy and radiation therapy due to the high radium content in the stone. Usually, however, it is best to avoid the heavily irradiated crystals, not because they are dangerous, but because the internal integrity of the stone is affected as a result of this form of microwave heat-processing.

Natural smoky quartz crystals absorb and neutralize harmful influences and shield the wearer from harm. This stone may also heighten our connection with the Earth as well as enhance our understanding of Nature and the environment.

TIGER'S EYE QUARTZ contains the gentle grounding energy of Earth. It is stabilizing and enduring and can help build confidence and increase one's sense of security. Tiger's Eye can help us to recognize our personal resources and use our abilities to attain our dreams because it is an excellent stone for developing and encouraging discipline and concentration, especially in children. This stone may bring abundance, prosperity and financial independence to the wearer.

Polished and set in copper, Tiger's Eye is powerful charm against harmful spirit intrusions. The brown, red and blue Tiger's Eye crystals are equally effective in their healing potencies.

TOURMALINATED QUARTZ contains black tourmaline inclusions. The essence of black tourmaline is magnified by this special stone (see TOURMALINE).

REALGAR

Crystal system: Monoclinic.

Cell salt: Arsenic sulfur.

Colour: Deep red to orange colour (may become yellow upon exposure to light).

Energy: Electromagnetic.

Element: Fire and water.

Planet/sign: Mars-Pluto; Venus-Neptune/Pisces.

Uses: Realgar is an enigmatic mineral because it is simultaneously crude and gentle. It can benefit those who wish to neutralize and refine their sexual energy.

RHODOCHROSITE

Crystal system: Hexagonal.

Cell salt: Manganese carbonate with some calcium, iron, magnesium and zinc.

Colour: Pink, rose-red, dark red, or brown.

Energy: Electric.

Element: Fire.

Planet/sign: Mercury-Uranus/Virgo; Jupiter/Sagittarius.

Uses: Rhodochrosite may be used to treat conditions affecting the upper respiratory system. It is an excellent blood purifier and may be worn at heart level to stimulate the circulation, or set in a copper bracelet.

Place Rhodochrosite crystal under your pillow at night to enhance and help you remember your dreams.

This stone is compatible with Malachite.

RHODONITE

Crystal system: Triclinic.

Cell salt: Manganese silicate, often with some calcium.

Colour: Brownish red, flesh-red and pink.

Energy: Electric.

Element: Earth and fire.

Planet/sign: Venus/Libra.

Uses: This stone may engender balance through strength of will. As a "karma" stone, it may also accelerate the inevitable consequences of cause and effect.

Pink Rhodonite helps us to monitor our thoughts, desires, words, actions and responses, while the brownish red and flesh red stones encourage self-discipline, stability, moral courage and faith.

RUTILE

Crystal system: Tetragonal.

Cell salt: Titanium dioxide, often with substantial amounts of iron.

Colour: Red, reddish brown, black.

Energy: Electric.

Element: Fire and earth.

Planet/sign: Mars-Pluto/Aries; Saturn/Capricorn.

Uses: Rutile both disciplines and structures our approach to life. It filters out painful memories and may be used when investigating the shadow side of the self.

SEA SHELLS

Crystal system: None.

Cell salt: Calcium phosphate with silica and other minerals which comprise the homes and skeletons of sea creatures.

Colour: Grey to white with opalescent pink, orange, yellow, white, blue and green (Abalone); red, pink, white, grey or black (Coral); white to yellow (Cowrie); opalescent white, cream, blue, grey to black (Pearl); red to orange with whitish pink (Spiny Oyster); brown to black, brownish green and brownish yellow (Tortoise).

Energy: Magnetic.

Element: Water.

Planet/sign: Moon; Cancer/Scorpio/Pisces.

Uses: Sea Shells symbolize boundless growth, emotions, hearing and the ear canals. Any shell may be carried to treat calcium deficiencies, mood disorders and bone diseases such as osteoporosis.

Sea Shells work well when combined with crystals, feathers, or other shamanic tools. They are especially useful to counterbalance overly dynamic energies due to their watery nature.

ABALONE, also known as Ear Shell, is found in warm tropical waters off the coasts of California, South America, Japan and China. This shell is commonly used for decorative purposes in jewellery. Some American Indians use the shell to hold spirit offering such as tobacco and blue corn. It also makes a great holder for burning sage, sweetgrass and cedar. Abalone may be helpful to build and protect the heart muscle as well as aid the digestion.

CORAL is found in oceans all over the world. Almost all cultures use Coral for reasons pertaining to magic, religion, or health. The ancients believed that those who carried red or white Coral could control the weather. Coral was thought to stop hemorrhaging and endow the wearer with wisdom.

The Indian people of the Southwestern United States make beautiful animal fetishes of Red Coral. Hindu healers use Red Coral as a blood purifier, claiming it can calm anger, jealousy and hatred when worn on the ring or index finger of the right hand. Black Coral is popular in the Caribbean for talismans and amulets to absorb negativity and protect the wearer from harm. Pink Coral is soothing, healing and pleasure-giving, while White Coral may be used to synchronize and stabilize the rhythms of the body-earth.

These lighter shades of Coral may become pale, which is a warning sign for the wearer of illness, weakened vitality, or toxicity.

In general, Coral is good for the bones and central nervous system, especially the brain stem. Because it quietens the emotions, it may be beneficial in the treatment of certain mental/emotional sickness.

When mixed with Diamond, Ruby, Emerald and Pearl and suspended at the entrance of a house, Coral makes a powerful amulet that will protect the dweller from harmful influences.

Peri-menopausal women may wear Red Coral to time ovulation and other cycles associated with the menses and to help regulate the hormones. The Coral fades when there is hormonal imbalance and brightens again when the hormones return to normal.

Coral should always be used in its whole and natural state for magical purposes.

COWRIE SHELL is most commonly used for decorative purposes, such as on ceremonial garments and jewellery. It may also be used as a spirit offering or in sympathetic magic wherein the energy of the sea is required.

PEARL is a round, calcified object produced in the bodies of oysters or other fresh or saltwater shellfish as a result of sand or some other foreign material irritating the creature's sensitive skin.

Pearls may be worn to purify the blood and to regulate body rhythms. For this reason, they are especially beneficial for pregnant or menopausal women. However, Pearls tend to absorb emotional energy. So please clear the stone before wearing it again if it has accompanied you into a negatively charged situation. Otherwise, Pearl is a soothing influence and can help you overcome obstacles.

A Pearl water tonic can be made to increase vitality, relieve eye strain and soothe burning urination. Place several small Pearls in water overnight and drink that water the following day. This tonic is a natural antacid and anti-inflammatory.

Pearl should be set in silver and worn on the right ring finger.

SPINY OYSTER contains the same medicinal properties as Red and Pink Coral; however, it is not as potent.

SERPENTINE

Crystal system: Monoclinic.

Cell salt: Basic magnesium silicates (Antigorite and Chrysolite).

Colour: Olive green, black to yellow-green, brown, yellow and white (rare); often with white streaks or striations.

Energy: Magnetic.

Element: Earth and water.

Planet/sign: Venus-Neptune/Pisces.

Uses: Italian streghe or witches believe that small pebbles of Serpentine offer protection from the bites of venomous creatures, mainly because the green colour streaked with white resembles snake skin. If a person has already been bitten by a snake or a poisonous insect, the stone is thought to draw out the toxins. These benefits may be had only if the stone is in its natural state and has never come into contact with iron.

Serpentine is also an excellent tool for psychic development, as it cleanses and conditions the emotions.

SMITHSONITE

Crystal system: Hexagonal.

Cell salt: Zinc carbonate, often with some iron.

Colour: White, grey, colourless, green, blue, yellow, purple, pink or brown.

Energy: Electric.

Element: Air and fire.

Planet/sign: Mercury/Virgo; Jupiter/Sagittarius.

Uses: Smithsonite helps us bring empowerment to action by enhancing our ability to complete desired goals. Also, use this stone to clarify the mind, instill a sense of security and ease difficulties in relationships.

SODALITE

Crystal system: Isometric.

Cell salt: Sodium aluminium silicate with chlorine.

Colour: Blue, grey, white, colourless or green, often streaked with white.

Energy: Electromagnetic.

Element: Air and water.

Planet/sign: Moon/Cancer; Mercury/Gemini; Saturn-Uranus/Aquarius.

Uses: Sodalite may be useful for balancing the metabolism. It is also a good shock absorber and may be used to combat the negative effects of radioactive materials and treatments, such as X-rays, radiation and chemotherapy.

Sodalite is a record-keeper and is easily impressed with new ideas and emotions. It is an excellent memory bank and can help you follow the track of previous incarnational experiences. Due to the sensitivity of the stone, new and previously unused crystals are best for personal use.

SPODUMENE

Crystal system: Monoclinic.

Cell salt: Lithium aluminium silicate.

Colour: White, grey, yellowish, emerald green (Hiddenite); pink to purple (Kunzite).

Energy: Magnetic.

Element: Water.

Planet/sign: Venus-Neptune/Pisces.

Uses: This stone suggests ideas associated with fertility, beauty, growth, depth and love.

> **HIDDENITE** *represents harmony through struggle and conflict. It has a definite affinity for Nature and the plant world. This stone teaches us to revere all our relations and to recognize our place in the scheme of all created things.*
>
> **KUNZITE** *has the interesting ability to absorb sunlight or artificial light and then give it off in the dark. Use it to relieve stress as well as to elicit feelings of love, compassion and good-will towards others.*
>
> *Due to its high lithium content, Kunzite crystal may also be used to balance certain biochemical disorders, such as schizophrenia and manic depression.*

STERCORITE

Crystal system: Triclinic.

Cell salt: Sodium phosphate.

Colour: White, colourless, yellow and brown masses or nodules.

Energy: Electric.

Element: Air.

Planet/sign: Venus-Neptune/Libra (exact cell salt equivalent) .

Uses: Stercorite increases knowledge and understanding through logic and reason. Use it when you need to make an important, impartial decision, as Stercorite allows for practical, objective, rational thinking, uncoloured by primal fear or emotions.

SUGILITE

Crystal system: Hexagonal.

Cell salt: Potassium sodium ferric lithium silicate.

Colour: Pale lavender to deep magenta or purplish black; sometimes streaked with green or white.

Energy: Magnetic.

Element: Water and earth.

Planet/sign: Mercury/Virgo; Jupiter/Sagittarius.

Uses: Sugilite is a powerful healing stone. The deep magenta stones may be used to heal painful emotions arising from repressed moodiness, hurt, resentment and anger. Streaked with green, Sugilite further soothes the untamed aspects of the instinctual nature, engendering forgiveness and protection. There are some indications that Sugilite can help ease the discomfort of migraine headaches when placed on the third eye or at the base of the skull. Polished Sugilite points are excellent transformational tools for releasing old habit patterns.

As Sugilite evolves, it will prove to be the most effective medicine in the alternative treatment of cancer as well as AIDS and other sexually transmitted diseases (STDs).

Sugilite is highly compatible with Turquoise, Red Coral, Onyx, Chrysoprase and Abalone.

SYLVANITE

Crystal system: Monoclinic.

Cell salt: Telluride of gold and silver; metallic.

Colour: Silver-white to steel grey.

Energy: Magnetic.

Element: Water.

Planet/Sign: Venus-Neptune/Pisces.

Uses: Sylvanite has tremendous conductive and transmissive capabilities because it contains both gold and silver. It engenders feelings of social conscience as well as heartfelt love and affection for humankind.

Hold Sylvanite in your receptive hand. Imagine that you are a tree. Your head is the top, your heart is the trunk and your feet are the roots, rooted in Mother Earth. Feel love well up in your heart. Send this love energy above, to Sky Father and below, to Earth Mother. Feel love returning to you from above and below, meeting in the middle, in your heart.

SYLVINE

Crystal system: Isometric.

Cell salt: Potassium chloride.

Colour: Yellow, blue or red.

Energy: Electric.

Element: Air.

Planet/sign: Gemini (exact cell salt equivalent); Jupiter/Cancer; Saturn-Uranus/Aquarius.

Uses: The cubic shapes formed by Sylvine represent stability, establishment, balance and permanence. This stone may be used when you are feeling nervous, upset or insecure.

THERNADITE

Crystal system: Orthorhombic.

Cell salt: Sodium sulphate.

Colour: White to brownish white or grey.

Energy: Magnetic and electric.

Element: Earth, fire and water.

Planet/sign: Venus/Taurus (exact cell salt equivalent); Sun/Leo; Mars-Pluto/Scorpio.

Uses: Thernadite crystal may be used to awaken and balance the throat, heart and belly centres. It is helpful for composing emotional upsets, soothing sore throats and abating heart palpitations due to anxiety.

Rub Thernadite crystal in a circular motion on the carotid artery located on the right and left sides of the neck for several minutes to quell a panic or anxiety attack.

TIGER'S EYE (SEE QUARTZ)

TOPAZ

Crystal system: Orthorhombic.

Cell salt: Aluminium fluorsilicate.

Colour: Colourless, pale, yellow-green, yellow to orange yellow, dark orange to red-orange; blue.

Energy: Electric.

Element: Air and fire.

Planet/Sign: Venus/Taurus; Mercury/Gemini; Jupiter/Sagittarius.

Uses: Topaz has long been considered as a Sun stone and may be used to increase vitality, strengthen the immune system and generally bring about good health. Set in gold, Topaz will protect the wearer from harm.

If you happen to channel spirit entities, Yellow Topaz is the stone for you. Clear Blue Topaz crystal enhances introspection. The colourless varieties of the stone bring wisdom and illumination. Green and yellow stones foster innocence and creative imagination, while Orange and Red Topaz may empower the wearer with courage and conviction.

Topaz should be worn in a gold necklace or on the right index finger in a gold ring.

1. TOURMALINE

Crystal system: Hexagonal.

Cell salt: Complex silicate of boron and aluminium; varied composition of inherent substances.

Colour: Pink and green (Elbaite and Watermelon Tourmaline); blue (Indicolite); red to purple-red

(Rubellite); dark orange-brown (Dravite); black; clear; Cat's Eye with inclusions.

Energy: Electromagnetic.

Element: Air, earth and fire.

Planet/sign: Mercury/Virgo; Jupiter/Sagittarius.

Uses: Tourmaline works to purify the entire body, including the auric field. It is a wonderful stress reducer, perhaps due to the sheer beauty of the stone. Worn on the person at heart level, Tourmaline conveys peace and tranquillity and helps organize scattered thoughts and emotions.

This stone is also well known for its ability to absorb tremendous amounts of negativity, both from the wearer and from the environment and it can make the wearer more sensitive to the immediate needs of the body-earth.

Black Tourmaline repels rather than absorbs negative energy. This stone is valuable during crises and situations causing emotional stress. It may be used to combat life-threatening diseases as well as to fight pyschic attack, spirit possession and harmful spirit intrusions.

Cat's Eye Tourmaline should only be used by those who are very attracted to it, as it seems to block energy rather than encourage it.

Clear Tourmaline is like a low-key Quartz. It works to cleanse and detoxify the immune system and may be useful in the treatment of eye problems and biochemical nerve disorders such as epilepsy.

DRAVITE *contains the essence of the Sun and the Earth. It is very helpful when worn while cultivating the garden.*

ELBAITE *crystallizes in both green and pink stones. The green crystal soothes an overly dynamic temperament, stimulates creativity and rejuvenates the body-earth. The pink stones enhance affection in difficult relationships and will help you to accept and love yourself. Pink or green Elbaite Tourmaline combined with Rose Quartz and set in silver is an excellent gift for lovers, life-mates, or close friends who need to rekindle love in their relationship.*

INDICOLITE *sublimates and heals discord, chaos, conflict, doubt and confusion.*

RUBELLITE *stimulates the will, the instincts and the memory. It can put us in touch with past life experiences, thus enabling us to better understand our motivations in this lifetime. It works to heal disturbing emotional influences that rise to the surface with no apparent cause. Large rubellite crystal formations may be kept in well-trafficked areas of homes where physical, verbal, or mental abuse is a common occurrence.*

WATERMELON TOURMALINE *will work to heal any situation where extreme conflict is a factor, as the combined pink and green colouration shows us how opposites work together in harmony to achieve beautiful result. Use this stone to anticipate which direction a particular situation is going to take, so that you may act accordingly.*

Watermelon Tourmaline has a strong affinity for green and growing things and is useful for inspiring a deep, abiding reverence for the natural beauty of the Earth.

2. TURQUOISE

Crystal system: Triclinic.

Cell salt: Hydrous basic phosphate of copper and aluminium, with some iron.

Colour: Sky blue, blue-green, apple-green, pale green and streak white.

Energy: Magnetic.

Element: Earth and air.

Planet/sign: Venus-Neptune/Libra.

Uses: Native Americans from New Mexico and Arizona carve Turquoise into animal shapes such as frogs, birds, squirrels, bears, coyotes and even porpoises and whales. The fetishes are usually strung together on a necklace and worn as a protective amulet. Turquoise is also a strong talisman for the hunter. A Turquoise tied to gun would ensure a swift and accurate kill.

Turquoise is very dependable health barometer. This stone tends to draw toxins from the body and is likely to fade or darken if you are harbouring disease in your system. I have seen this many times and sometimes the effects are quite dramatic.

A friend of mine suffered from chronic skin inflammations due to an early, life-threatening illness. Whenever a portion of her skin had any problem, her Turquoise ring, which was normally coloured light blue-green, would turn to a dark forest green colour. When the condition cleared up, the ring would return to its original shade.

This stone can also be used to cure illness: the Shoshone Indians use Turquoise and Jade together under water and send prayers to heal a sick mind or body.

Hindu mystics say Turquoise brings wealth if you look at it on the first day after the new Moon. The Navajos have a similar idea (previously mentioned in chapter 7) involving Turquoise and a coyote, a trickster with decidedly lunar tendencies.

Turquoise may be offered in friendship, as the spirit in the stone is quite amiable about transferring allegiance from one person to another.

In general, Turquoise is wonderful for healing, protection and self-definition. This stone really lets you know who you are.

3. VIVIANITE

Crystal system: Monoclinic.

Cell salt: Hydrous phosphate of iron.

Colour: Blue, green, or colourless when freshly excavated, but darkens when exposed to light.

Energy: Magnetic.

Element: Water.

Planet/sign: Venus-Neptune/Pisces (exact cell salt equivalent).

Uses: Vivianite regulates the delicate endocrine system. It aids us in defending the body-earth against disease by instilling in us a positive mental outlook on life. This stone may be useful for treating severe depression and as a preventative medicine when the body is threatened by illness as a result of long-term, negative mental and emotional state of consciousness.

WULFENITE

Crystal system: Triclinic.

Cell salt: Lead molybdate.

Colour: Yellow, orange, brown and yellowish grey.

Energy: Electric.

Element: Air.

Planet/sign: Venus-Neptune/Libra.

Uses: Wulfenite stimulates blood circulation and carries light-energy throughout the body-earth. Owing to its high lead content, Wulfenite may be used during meditation to focus healing energy on specific body areas.

ZIRCON

Crystal System: Tetragonal.

Cell salt: Zirconium silicate, often with some hafnium.

Colour: Grey, brown and green; transparent red (Hyacinth); and colourless or smoky (Jargoon).

Energy: Electromagnetic.

Element: Fire and earth.

Planet/sign: Mars/Aries; Saturn/Capricorn.

Uses: This stone helps us synthesize our action so that we become focused to accomplish our goals.

Conclusion

I hope the readers may find the descriptions of the selection of Gems through various methods very useful. Wearing the appropriate gem does wonders in solving the problems, offers protection from the evil influences of planets and enhances their beneficial effect.

In this book, I have described about the choice of appropriate gem stones for different people born in different Zodiac signs, stars, months and dates.

Of all the methods of selecting gem stones, the best and perfect method is selecting through one's date of birth. Because planets work on numbers and colours very efficiently than in any other ways to get the maximum benefits. I have also described the auspicious dates, days and time, for wearing each gem and the rituals to be performed on each gem stone, so that the good vibrational powers of the particular gem may be captured in the ring.

You can take the advice of a professional gemmologist to select the most beneficial gems.

V. RAJSUSHILA

www.ingramcontent.com/pod-product-compliance
Lightning Source LLC
Chambersburg PA
CBHW070335230426
43663CB00011B/2324